Busking the Gospel

Ordained Ministry in Secular Employment

— J A M E S M. M. F R A N C I S —

Sacristy
Press

Sacristy Press
PO Box 612, Durham, DH1 9HT

www.sacristy.co.uk

First published in 2021 by Sacristy Press, Durham

Sacristy Limited, registered in England & Wales, number 7565667

British Library Cataloguing-in-Publication Data
A catalogue record for the book is available from the British Library

ISBN 978-1-78959-155-2

Contents

Foreword

After centuries of ordaining young men to the priesthood which paid and housed them for life, thus freeing them not to spend time in other paid employment, in the twentieth century the Church of England, along with its sister denominations, finally asked itself important and long-overdue questions about whether this model was still appropriate as the only way for people to follow a vocation to ordained ministry.

Since then developments have been, at times, a little haphazard. However, over the years, in addition to encouraging the ordination of older people and opening ordained ministry to women, the churches have nurtured the vocations of people for whom ordained ministry embraces their daily work in other fields. For decades, this ministry in the Church of England was defined by what people are not ("non-stipendiary ministers") rather than what they are. Gradually the nomenclature "self-supporting ministers" was introduced, but the emphasis was still on financial arrangements and it is only recently that the much more positive "minister in secular employment" (MSE) has been more widely adopted, although—as this book explains—even this is not ideal. But at last the emphasis is on the fact that people are ministers, followed by the description of where they express much of their ministry, rather than beginning with the lack of payment by the Church, which always seems to imply that a person's secular employment is a financial necessity rather than part of their vocation and thus a gift to the Church.

As Jim Francis describes in this book, the roots of this ministry lie in various places and, while the MSE plant that is growing in the Church of England owes something to all of them, what is emerging is slightly different and needs its own grounding in the Church's theology and ecclesiology held alongside the social, political and economic realities of the world today. Until now, there has been little written that specifically explores this expression of the vocation to ordained ministry, which may account for continuing confusion within the Church and the difficulty for some people in discerning a call to this vocation. This book will make a welcome and significant contribution to remedying that deficit.

MSE is part of the total ministry of the Church and is neither a replacement for anything (other forms of ordained ministry or lay ministries like Readers) nor appropriate for everyone. Instead, it is another expression of our sharing, as baptized Christians, in the ministry that Christ has entrusted to the Church. First and foremost, we are called, through baptism, to share in the Trinitarian life of God as expressed in our world through Creation, the Incarnation and the Pentecostal outpouring of the Holy Spirit. Flowing from that, we are called to work with God's continuing action for the transformation of the world, which has as a prerequisite, Spirit-guided, incarnational engagement with the world, expressed in part through our work. We do well to remember, as is explored in depth in the Excursus, that God worked at Creation and Jesus' public ministry was essentially an early expression of MSE: he was a carpenter-builder, and his disciples had working backgrounds to which the Gospels indicate they returned at times until, after the resurrection, they were sent further afield as apostles. Even then, some early Christian missionaries earned their income; St Paul worked as a tentmaker alongside Priscilla and Aquila.

This book focuses on MSE, but, in doing so, it is about far more than that. It contains wisdom on ministry and ordination and on work which all Christians would benefit from absorbing. As Jim Francis writes, "Far from being at the edge of the Church as a form of ministry, MSE is actually somewhere at the centre of what the Church is about in a vision of the gospel and purposeful living" (p. 59). Would that the Church could grasp more firmly that vision of the interface of the gospel and daily living. I remember a residential weekend, when I was training people for ordination, on the theme of ethics, in which some ordinands gave presentations about ethics in their very different workplaces. It was stunning to hear their exemplary and visionary ethical engagement with their work, and if ever there was an argument for MSE, they were it: their insights and experience were a vital gift not only for their worshipping communities but for their employers and colleagues and could have been gained only because they were fully immersed as theologically resourced

Christians in their (very varied) worlds of work. After ordination some of them were to remain in their workplaces as MSEs and their vocation and gifting for this was evident.

Jim Francis is well qualified to write about ministry in secular employment, having served in that capacity for forty-five years, first as a minister of the Church of Scotland and, since 1987, in the Church of England. Over the years, Jim has expressed his ordained ministry through his work in education at a polytechnic/university, diocesan ministry courses and a school. For eighteen years, he was the Bishop of Durham's Advisor on Self-Supporting Ministry. He says of himself that all his adult career has been an interweaving of teaching and ministry which have always gone together for him. Over the years that I have known Jim, I have valued his quiet, humbly offered insights and example, and I am delighted that his wisdom born of forty-five years of MSE will be shared more widely through this book.

The Revd Canon Rosalind Brown
Canon Emerita, Durham Cathedral
Author of Being a Deacon Today *and co-author of* Being a Priest Today

Introduction

Where is the place of God's glory? Blessed is the
Lord whose glory is revealed in every place.

Jewish Prayer Book[1]

The purpose of this book is to contribute to reflection on a form of Christian ministry called ministry in secular employment (MSE). MSEs are self-supporting (mostly but not exclusively ordained as deacon or priest), with a particular vocational focus on how their ministry encompasses their places of employment or other non-church contexts. Titles and acronyms are rarely wholly satisfactory. While MSE refers to ministers in secular employment, many such clergy prefer to call themselves ministers in secular environment since it may encompass the experience of unemployment. Moreover, for almost all such clergy the word "secular" is itself unsatisfactory since all creation belongs to God and nothing is really secular.[2] However, for now, we will retain the description (acronym), leaving open whether the "e" means employment (including self-employment) or environment.

Ministry is also something of a challenge to define given the rediscovery of collaborative ministry and the still underacknowledged contribution to faith and witness of Christians in their daily lives.[3] After all, baptism is our common shared authority for discipleship and ministry, and all ministry flows from discipleship. And let it be affirmed that there is also a feminine form of the word "disciple" in the New Testament (*mathétria*, Acts. 9.36). However, as a working approach we shall use discipleship for the calling of the whole people of God to witness and service within the one ministry or high priesthood of Christ. And we shall discuss MSE within the representative ordained ministry of the Church. Historically, self-supporting ministry (SSM) emerged through, and developed from, a particular vocation to ordained ministry in secular employment. As this self-supporting (earlier called non-stipendiary) ministry has evolved and grown, that original MSE vision has become somewhat occluded by the number of SSMs who are in effect voluntary parish clergy—truly auxiliary pastoral ministers, as one of the original titles mooted for SSM described it. Whilst appreciative of self-supporting ministry in general, there is arguably a need to reaffirm the distinctive focus of MSE.

At the outset, it may be helpful to set MSE in the context of the Church's understanding of ordained ministry, and then to say some things that are important for the nurturing of a vocation to MSE that arise from it. If the frequency of mention is on priesthood, this is not to overlook the distinctive diaconate, and it may be that diaconal ministry is particularly vocationally significant for MSE. The Sixth International Anglican Liturgical Consultation in Berkeley, California in 2001 defined ordained ministry as follows: "In order that the whole people of God may fulfil their calling to be a holy priesthood, serving the world by ministering Christ's reconciling love in the power of the Spirit, people are ordained to enable others to fulfil their calling."

The MSE will consciously include work and a commitment to it as an ordained minister in this calling and shaped by this context. In this ministry, "being there" in the representative significance of ordained ministry is given a key emphasis. It reflects a vocation to ordained ministry in being called into one's work rather than out of it in the awareness of the ordained minister as public person. That is to say, the ordained minister's public role is not confined to the Church, even though it may be within the Church that it receives its most immediate recognition. In such ways as these, MSE is especially open to pushing the boundaries of the meaning of a representative ministry.

Such ordained ministry is thus to be expressed holistically alike in worship and in work. Indeed a positive gain is made of the fact that this ministry has a social as well as a church dimension in reflecting the priesthood of Christ that embraces world and Church.[4] Michael Ramsey speaks of priesthood and the priesthood of Christ with reference to the letter to the Hebrews 7:25 thus:

> But we may go deeper, and when we do so we find the concept of
> the interceding high priest simpler still. When we say "he lives to

make intercession for us", we note the verb *entugchanein*, which we habitually translate "intercede", means literally not to make petitions or indeed to utter words at all but to meet, to encounter, to be with someone on behalf of or in relation to others. Jesus is with the Father; with him in the intimate response of perfect humanity; with him in the power of Calvary and Easter; with him as one who bears us all upon his heart, our Son of Man, our friend, our priest; with him as our own. That is the continuing intercession of Jesus the high priest.

It is as Ramsey describes it "to be with God with the people on our heart", and we need not and should not limit "people" to the members of a congregation.[5] Perhaps other themes of ordained ministry have been emphasized since Ramsey's time of writing, but they do not make invalid this great insight. Of course that means an intercessory association both with those who do not go near the church, and with others who do, away from the particular context of a congregation. That is also true of stipendiary ministers, not least parish clergy. With that in mind, John Rodwell offers a salutary comment:

> That is the challenge of an incarnational religion, to make present in our own flesh, through the substance of what the world gives us, a realization of God's activity in his creation, trying to hold together what sin would pull apart. Frankly, I have found that whether people carry conviction in this way as Christians has nothing to do with whether they are stipendiary or NSM, ordained or lay . . . Surprisingly, then, I find myself blessed—and, of course, that discovery is the start and finish of the Christian life.[6]

Nevertheless here it belongs in that non-quantifiable reckoning of, and vocation to, an "habituated presence" in the workplace (actual or online) which the MSE has with others as a colleague.

A further significant point is not only how the individual perceives their ministry but whether priesthood has any meaning in society generally. In other words, the social and societal contexts of ministry are profoundly important. MSE affords its own distinctive perspective for ordained ministry as a *public person* in the workplace. Through a patient ministry at work established over a length of time, a community within the public space of work will come to matter to the MSE as much as the community of the church, even though the shape of this ministry will be different from that of the church community: one that is often indirect, never to be taken for granted, continuously being reminted, and always dependent on a contextual meaning of reception. It will come to be the case that an MSE will be at home in two places, of work and church, and thereby will know as well the discomfort of not being completely at home in either for the advantage of both. In all of this, the challenges of improvising, indeed of busking one's ministry come into play.

There are today some signs of a reinvigoration of MSE as the numbers of SSM candidates declare an MSE-focused ministry, just as there has been a significant increase in reflection on the ways in which daily life (and work) contribute to Christian discipleship. However, in ministry training, the theological exploration of MSE is almost non-existent. Very few courses, if any, devote a module or part of a training course to this subject. As a consequence, MSEs are left to work out a theological rationale for themselves. That many do, and that much theological reflection is to be found in the literature and recorded experience of MSE, is surely affirmative of just how resilient and thoughtful the practitioners of this ministry have been and are. So there is a body of evidence to turn to. However, apart from some key books,[7] much of it exists in articles, pamphlets, short essays, letters and diaries. This makes it difficult to access study material readily for the purposes both of training, and of sustaining ongoing reflection for those who have a vocation to MSE.

This book seeks to encourage and affirm those who are exploring a vocation to, and those who have embraced, this form of ministry, as deacon and priest. It takes up the metaphor of busking, as a means to understanding some key themes theologically, missionally and formationally attendant upon its varied forms of expression. It would thereby wish to remind the Church of the contribution that MSEs make through their ministry within the structures and opportunities of working life, and to value some key perspectives that inform and shape ministry in secular employment. To that end those who rightly advocate for MSE recognize that at a fundamental level this is not only about a particular form of ministry but how the Church engages with the world of work generally. The book begins by reviewing self-supporting ministry in relation to the emergence of MSE.

Chapter 2 introduces and explores the image of busking as a way of conveying the improvisatory nature of MSE. It identifies four features of a busking style illustrative of MSE and finds these reflected in the ministry of Jesus.

Chapters 3 and 4 then take up the improvisatory nature of MSE in addressing and responding to the fundamental dimensions of the Church's life in Christ, which are discipleship, ministry, human fulfilment and sociality.

Chapter 5 explores how MSE draws mission and accountability together in fruitful ways of commending this ministry within the Church. Chapter 6 returns to the four characteristics of a busking style to show how these inform and shape the formational nature of MSE. It is in this chapter that the metaphor of busking illustrative of MSE finds its true home.

If the reader wishes simply to gain a succinct appreciation of MSE, then Chapters 2 and 6 may be read together. The conclusion offers some brief summative outcomes in valuing MSE. An excursus explores the relationship in Christian origins between a supported and a self-supporting ministry and suggests that they are more complementary than might at first appear.

MSE deserves a theological focus in its own right because it involves a number of themes that go to the very heart of the gospel and the purpose of the Church. This is not to claim for MSE more than its due. But it is to recognize the issues and opportunities that it raises. These questions arise from time to time in the story of the emergence of MSE in the modern age, but as often as not become occluded or domesticated back into the traditional life of the Church. Nevertheless, these questions persist and will not go away. Attending to them is what belongs within the practice of MSE and its invitation to an inherent kind of improvisation.

To begin with a personal story, and it is noteworthy how often ministers in secular employment draw upon narrative to express and explain their ministry, I was at very short notice, and quite unexpectedly, made redundant.[8] It proved a traumatic experience. Leaving aside some of the obvious economic and personal aspects, there was the realization that for better or worse I had lost a ministry. This grieved me, though that was not in any way a concern for my (former) employer. After all, I was not there as a chaplain. Nor, however, was the Church very much concerned at least in institutional terms, since I was not drawing a stipend for my ministry, and my licence as a priest was not affected. So two of my familiar structures carried on—the one (my place of work) without me, in which I had hitherto found my centre and in which I had been at home, and the other (the Church) still with me but without a personal centre of vocation. What remains with me, as a longer-term reflection from that time, were some conversations. For example, my work colleagues sympathetically considered that I had a second string to my bow, as it were, and the Church would "see me right for a job". They were taken aback when I said it did not work like that, and the Church was under no obligation to give me a living. Nor indeed did I think or wish to ask for one, since stipendiary ministry is not the refuge of the unemployed. And the staff at the job centre were mystified when I tried to explain the mysteries of self-supporting ministry, that there could ever be such a thing as "an unemployed vicar"!

I mention all this because whilst I have long reflected on the nature of self-supporting ministry,[9] the experience of losing a job caused me to think afresh about MSE, and what precisely it is that has held and continues to hold an attraction about an ordained ministry shaped in this way. It represents a small but significant contribution to the complex mosaic of how the Church engages with the world in response to the call and mission of the gospel. We need a deeper sense of how we see this in ourselves as a whole, something that actually goes beyond the confines of the work context, however significant our commitment to work. But it is also clear how little the Church prepares clergy for such a ministry at work as this and supports them in it. Preparation for self-supporting ministry will by and large not be that much different from stipendiary ministry. But ministry in secular employment, although it stands under the broad description of SSM, is different in some important respects. And it should command the attention of the Church generally and of training programmes in particular, far more than it does. The Church has scarcely taken to heart the words of Roland Allen writing as long ago as 1922 (and of course before the ordination of women):

There is an idea that if men engaged in ordinary trades and business and professions were ordained they would necessarily be part-time priests, and by that word part-time men mean that they would be priests when they were in Church and laymen when they were out of it. A priest can never be anything but a priest. There should be no obstacle in the exhortation in the ordinal to priests to apply themselves wholly to this one thing and to draw all their worldly care and studies this way. Every act of life ought to be an act worthy of a priest of God, and if men engaged in professions and trades were ordained . . . and carried on their trade or profession as men who were called with a holy calling, they would not only get into real vital touch with men who cannot understand what it means to be a priest, but they would learn and teach us a new conception of the relation of religion and daily life.[10]

This quotation, with its enduring relevance, raises a number of important issues, which, despite the subsequent acceptance in the Church of England of ministers in secular employment, still hover around this form of ministry and obstinately refuse to go away. That process and its struggle are a reflection not on the validity of an MSE form of ministry but on the narrowness of the Church's vision. Despite Allen's point, these self-supporting clergy are sometimes still called part-time as if all that actually mattered was service to God within the ecclesiastical framework of the Church. This form of ministry can and should make a renewed contribution to a better understanding within Christian discipleship of the relationship between faith, world and Church in affirming the emergent presence of God's kingdom. By God's grace as Creator and Redeemer the created order may and will forever participate in the holiness of God. That is part at least of what Christians affirm in the Incarnation and Resurrection of Christ, the worship of God which acknowledges and celebrates the undying and undeniable worthship that the world has in the will and purpose of God. In this sense, the world in its secularity is also holy, not by acquiring some new power of its own, but by being held by, re-established through, and brought to completion in a right relationship with God.

CHAPTER 1

Setting the Scene

MSE is in part influenced by what the Church expects of these clergy who are self-supporting through employment. In other words, since the Church does not appoint MSEs to their work, but receives this as a gift in recognizing a work-based ministry, the Church must take a significant responsibility in both supporting MSEs and in helping them to shape their ministry. One definition of MSE, amongst several, is the following:

> The purpose of MSE is to deepen the vocation of the whole Church to serve Christ in the world, and to be a representative sign of the presence in the world of the mystery of God.[11]

This two-fold conjoined focus expresses very well the representative and mediatorial vocation of ordained ministry, rooted in the representative and mediatorial life of the whole Church. It is this that, whatever else is to be said, gives MSE a secure theological rationale and foundation.[12] Broadening this out, MSEs are:

1. An affirmation of the creativity of people in being one with God's purposeful activity in faith and hope.
2. Models for other Christians caught up in complexities and compromises.
3. Those who have a particular opportunity to affirm the work of all who struggle for justice and peace, wholeness and healing.[13]
4. Priests of God's creation in bringing his world to him in prayer and worship, particularly in the offering of the Eucharist. As one MSE observed, "I do not carry a cross in my work jacket but a slide rule in my cassock pocket."[14]

5. Those who establish a clear relationship between the work context and the mission of the Church in the vocation of all God's people.

In exploring this vocation, a set of personal questions begins to emerge: [15]

1. What in work has nurtured my calling to remain within it, in a commitment to its context, as an ordained MSE?
2. What insights of faith do I bring to addressing the relationship between purpose and people in the workplace?
3. What do my own gifts and abilities at work as a person contribute to shaping my understanding of ordained ministry?
4. What do I want to explore in my faith as it relates to work (as a sort of SWOT analysis)?
5. How can I nurture others through their work?
6. How can I so appreciate work that it contributes to who I am, but without consuming me?

The history of self-supporting ministry in modern times reflects a process of adaptation and improvisation as the Church's understanding of ministry engaged with the world.[16] As noted earlier, the original impetus for self-supporting ministry came from MSE even though the predominant profile of self-supporting ministry has moved to auxiliary parish ministry. In the emergence of the Southwark Ordination Course (1963), it was thought that it would be good to have ministers whose experience and expertise was in the world of work and who at the same time would contribute to the life and worship of the (local) church. As this initiative grew and developed, the relationship to the world of work has proved more variable than the relationship to the Church. Marcus Thompson-McCausland (MSE and garage mechanic) reflects on moving from stipendiary ministry:

> A few asked why "I had left the ministry", but my aim was to enter it in a new/old way. It is about setting aside status and seeking the stature of Christ after the manner of Philippians chapter 2, the self-emptying of Christ in the Incarnation. Our divine Brother and Lord so far discarded his divine status that he was crucified

naked between two thieves. In descending he cast away status;
in ascending he ascended with true human stature, and this was
his "gift unto humankind". Status is outward, stature is inward.
Status is jealous, stature generous. I do not claim to have made
the exchange; I have glimpsed the necessity and dipped a toe
in the water, no more. But because I perceive that the church
must teach it, I must of necessity try to do it myself. That is the
best explanation I can so far offer of why I stopped being an
incumbent and put on overalls. I "signed on" and soldiered on
and everything blessed me . . . The ministry was similar in that
I was again an honorary curate and self-supporting . . . Now I
was quite plainly a servant. More of the ear than the tongue was
required on my part, but I carried chrism as well as Castrol.[17]

There are some self-supporting clergy who have a job, but this is primarily
regarded as a source of income. No doubt they recognize and affirm a
general Christian presence and discipleship in the world of work and
will seek to be participant in it (acknowledging that work informs their
faith as much as faith informs their work). However, their sense of
vocation (in being formally recognized as a minister) exists in the Church
rather than at work. It may be that some would wish to be a stipendiary
minister but for one reason or another are not able to realize that focus
of ministry. Then there are those, let us recognize them as MSEs, who
will intentionally seek to draw the workplace into an ordained ministry.
Questions about role and recognition are perceived as less urgent and
are more indirect. In this model, "being there", in the representative
significance of ordained ministry, is given a key emphasis. And as a
corollary of this, an emphasis is also placed on the assertion that ordained
ministry is not to be reduced to, nor measured by, a set of functions
(usually as an invidious comparison with parish ministry).

   To mention a further complexity, there are some MSEs who may
be invited to take on an informal or even formal chaplaincy role in
the workplace (sometimes referred to in USA contexts as "corporate
chaplaincy"), and are appointed for a recognized provision of pastoral
care. This would be akin to an Industrial Mission/sector ministry model,
although the person continues to be a working employee of the company

or institution. Perhaps we might identify those MSEs who have such a formal chaplaincy at work, in addition to being employed, as having a *work-place ministry* to distinguish this from a *work-based ministry*.[18]

Any study of MSE requires some recognition of the witness of the worker priest movement. John Mantle draws a distinction between MSE and worker priests (primarily on the basis of the latter's focus on manual labour).[19] However, he goes on to say:

> MSEs, while maintaining a relationship with their parish church and its incumbent, see their ministry focused in their place of work, be it school, shop, lab or factory. They enter—in the face of the Church's public faith and public failings—with substantial theological comprehension, pastoral know-how and an authoritative sign and voice because they are ordained.[20]

And he further notes:

> Nevertheless ministers in secular employment have some affinity with worker priests. They often understand their role as rooted in incarnational theology. It is about the Church—in the person of the ordained clergy—supporting the laity at work, or remaining, perhaps permanently, in environments where there may be no Christians. The MSE's daily environment is "other people's territory", often alien and hostile. This is a unique ministry and deserves to be recognized and encouraged in a special way.

Mantle elsewhere suggests that the ordained in the workplace are able to offer "an understanding of human and pastoral problems, substantial theological comprehension, and a human face for a distant institution whose clergy (s)he represents."[21]

This is recognized even in Ordained Local Ministry. One says "even" since the idea that a local ministry might actually embrace a place of work gets a mention only in passing. From *Stranger in the Wings* 3.21 (at the time of this Report OLM was called Local Non-Stipendiary Ministry—LNSM):

As we have seen earlier in this chapter, all Christians are called to live out the gospel in every aspect of their daily lives. LNSMs, by virtue of their non-stipendiary ordained ministry, share with lay Christians the task of Christian witness not just in the local community but in the world of work. It would be quite wrong to assume that it is only NSMs in the broader category who are well placed to explore the pressures, opportunities and ethical questions that arise in the workplace, whereas LNSMs are people concerned more narrowly with the gathered Christian community. On the contrary, LNSMs will be well placed, within the local church, to share with others in reflecting upon how people are to be supported in their wider lives and how best the local church may give proper space and attention to such issues.[22]

However, the subsequent recorded experiences in this report are such as to nuance the experience of work away from the work setting to the church setting. Alongside this there is also noted i) the frustration of being able to minister in only one place—"From being a Reader where I could be mobile, becoming an OLM has proved restrictive";[23] and ii) a feeling that for some becoming an OLM has made them dissatisfied with their "bread and butter job".[24] So clearly OLM experience has had some impact on the work environment, but the evidence, such as it is, is rather ambiguous.

The accountability to the Church for the MSE's ministry is one that transcends roles even though the latter are significant.[25] A creative perspective here (on which see further below[26]) is to find in accountability the underlying notion of giving an account i.e. the Church should be eager to hear, nurture and support the stories of such a ministry as this. And this narrative meaning of accountability engages with how all that flourishes in human life can be drawn into a kingdom or an incarnational structured theology.[27] R. T. France makes a telling point that we do well not to shorten the phrase "kingdom of God" to simply "kingdom" (though it is difficult not to do this). "If the 'Kingdom of God' means 'God being King', then to abbreviate to 'the Kingdom' is to focus on the wrong one of the two nouns."[28] It addresses itself fully to the claim of the presence of God in all things, the reality of who God is in that one characteristic, as we experience it, of God as reigning. Again, one of the consequences of the Christian doctrine of Incarnation is that, whatever else, God's Being is knowable, expressed in personal form in Jesus Christ, and so the knowability of God is to be found in who we are amid the circumstances of life.

Evidence for the experience of MSE, on which to draw for theological interpretation, is to be found in a number of essays, articles and book length studies. Evidence also exists more widely in pamphlets and documents with limited circulation. One of the most wide-ranging collections of stories and commentary upon them is to be found in *Working for the Kingdom: The Story of Ministers in Secular Employment*, a book edited by J. Fuller and P. Vaughan and published in 1986.[29]

A survey of the experience of MSEs from these stories tends to reflect three contexts, though these are not to be understood as being exclusive to each other. Running through them all is the underlying sense that for all the variety there is a vision that feels holistic and coherent even though it may not necessarily be readily explainable. They remind us also of the significance of how others may serve as a guide or inspiration for one's own ministry. The three contexts are the MSE within the Church, the relationship between workplace and Church, and the MSE within the workplace.

Within the Church

In relation to the Church, MSEs will inevitably experience some tensions in all probability being known at work as a minister, whilst, by and large, the overt liturgical dimension to that ministry is elsewhere in "another community". They will realize that they have been selected as (ordained) ministers of the Church and not primarily for what their ministry is at work, however significant the latter is for them. They will also often feel that they have little input into the decision-making structures of the Church. On the other hand, they may well sense that MSE taps into a natural sort of priesthood anyway that others recognize, a ministry in the workplace that is embedded in the implicit, or even explicit, acceptance in secular contexts of the idea of a naturally existing priesthood.[30] This suggests that for many MSEs a vocation to ordination is perhaps more a matter of uncovering rather than discovering a vocation. It also gives a different, but no less important, understanding of this as a public ministry compared with how that is traditionally articulated by the Church. The issue then is how such a ministry is sacralized, and this in turn raises issues relating to the other two contexts.

Between work and Church

Apart from some occasional perceived differences between roles and authority, and even (for some) between status and style, MSEs will be well aware of, and generally adept at handling, challenges in balancing commitment to the job, responsibilities in life and obligations to the Church as licensed ministers. This is more than simply a management issue of using time and resources carefully. Indeed the approach of balancing is perhaps not the best way of expressing this, since it tends to imply working with two discrete entities. MSEs will look instead for integration, and the ways in which various responsibilities can be opportunities for influencing each other and for mutual enrichment. This is no easy task. Paul Watson (MSE and professor of veterinary physiology) recalls:

> My concern is the lack of continuity between my local church ministry and my secular employment. While I try to be the one person in both settings, the local congregation finds it virtually impossible to conceive that I have a secular life. My College colleagues are aware of my church commitments, but largely are merely impressed with my stamina! However, I remain sustained by the belief that, although His activities cannot always be discerned, God works in the secret places of the heart. As interpreter I work with the clergy and the laity interpreting the one to the other, convincing the clergy that the stresses of working life are real; and I represent to the laity a model of involvement with the life of the local church from where they are in the world of work.[31]

The often-used metaphors of being a "two-way street" or "a bridge" signal the importance for MSEs of encouraging and nurturing others within the Church in their ministry in the world.[32] For this to be effective, MSE needs paradoxically to work with a theology of the Church as much as a theology of work,[33] including one that will enable the Church to appreciate more widely a doctrine of creation as well as redemption.[34] But what would it mean to rediscover the Church embedded in the idea of creation? Not surprisingly it would require a rethinking of redemption away from the predominant tacit assumption of rescue from the world. It is to be made anew in the image of God.

The Church consequently has to broaden its thinking about the meaning of redemption and its own birthright in the gospel of Christ's cross and resurrection, in light of creation. It takes up what Paul says that "all things have been created through him and for him" and about all things holding together in Christ (Colossians 1:16–17). The Church born out of the life, death and resurrection of Jesus is not a starting over again on some other ground or in some place other than the created order. What Paul calls a new creation (Galatians 6:15; 2 Corinthians 5:17) is just that—to use the distinction in the Greek of the New Testament, it is not new as "another" ("*neos*") but "made new" ("*kainos*"), that is to say, it is not about another creation but creation renewed. We return to the idea not so much that MSEs in and of themselves are ministers of the kingdom, but that indeed the Church itself in Christ is minister of the kingdom. What MSEs must do is to save the Church from amnesia, and it is that which is a prophetic and a pastoral task.[35] MSE is not just about how a gap between Church and world might be "bridged". It is more fundamental than that, not least in challenging the Church to reflect more fully on its own meaning and identity.

Within work

The work context itself raises a number of issues, including visiting anew the meaning of ordination. Conceding the valid point that one does not need to be ordained to do the work that one is doing, a vocation to remain in the workplace nevertheless informs and shapes the MSE's calling as an ordained minister. And, we should add, why not? It is to be looked for and expected, and indeed affirmed. Nevertheless, this does raise a fundamental point about what it is to be ordained. The answer to that may very likely be diverse, with some putting an emphasis on function and others on presence. The latter was an answer given by some in the French worker priest movement, and echoed by MSEs, about "being there".

It has to be pointed out, however, that the ecclesiology underlying the French WP idea of "*présence*" cannot readily be transposed, for example, into Anglicanism since the WP idea is informed by the Roman Catholic notion that the Church is present fully only in its eucharistic celebration, and thereby centred on its priesthood. Therefore "*présence*" is assured by Roman Catholic worker priests in a way that is not implied in the Anglican tradition in its ecclesiological understanding of the priesthood of the Church rooted in baptism. Whilst the French WPs did not have "a single developed theology for life and work",[36] the Roman Catholic understanding of ordination clearly shaped their focus on the meaning of Incarnation i.e. it is the Eucharist that makes the Church, and therefore the WPs in working amongst the labouring classes were constituting the Church in their midst.

For Anglicanism, the Reformation influence of the understanding of ordination is one in which the ordained nurture the whole people of God in their share in the priesthood of Christ. If occasional arguments are still mistakenly made that ordained ministry in the workplace disables the ministry of the laity, this adds significant pressure to explain MSE. One suspects, however, that this view is informed by a somewhat particular (role-based) perception of ordained ministry that MSEs themselves may not share. Moreover, as we have already noted, across the whole history of the Church there have been clergy who have earned a living rather than received a stipend. It is very obvious that they have not hindered the ministry and witness of the whole people of God, and as likely as not they have enhanced it.

Very likely, then, there is nothing distinctive about the role of the ordained minister in secular employment as "worker person". Does this then leave the MSE as a sort of distinctive parish-based minister rather than a specialized ordained workplace minister?[37] But perhaps this does not get to the heart of the matter in terms of what ordination is as something holistic and not to be reduced to the question of function and role. If vocation is not something coterminous with role but arguably belongs to the creativity of who we are as human beings,[38] then this enables MSEs to connect with the idea of ministry at work in a way that is deeper and wider than balancing roles in work and Church. So the description of MSEs as "part-time" is really a misnomer.

There is something fundamental here that is worth teasing out, which is about the public nature of ordained ministry generally. In the perception of ordained ministry, it is as well to distinguish between a public perception, an administrative precision and a theological appreciation. These three hover around the discourse of ordination:

- **Public perception:** vicar
- **Church administrative precision:** acronyms for stipendiary, non-stipendiary, ordained local minister, bi-vocational minister
- **Theological appreciation:** bishop, priest, deacon

The public perception of the ordained is broadly that of a "vicar" without too much concern for the niceties of context. The administrative mind of the Church addresses necessary nuances in relation to the diversity of (ordained) ministry e.g. incumbency, non-stipendiary ministry and local ministry. And then undergirding all, are the theological foundations of what it means to be a deacon, priest or bishop. The difficulty is where things in, say, the administrative layer become transported into the theological layer and then back to their shaping in the public perception, within which clergy then feel compelled to articulate distinctions.

This is where a difficulty can arise for MSEs over the Church's wish for employer working agreements and the difficulty of an employer agreeing to that.[39] Moreover, in truth, the very such mention of the place of work arguably skews the significance of how diaconal and priestly ministry encompasses all of one's life context(s). Or again, to return to an earlier point, it also becomes the case that the theological passion for a diaconal and priestly engagement with God's world rises into the institutional discernment processes. It then becomes categorized, with the consequent debate about whether a ministry at work devalues the ministry of the laity—though again it should be said that it is to discipleship that we are all primarily called by our baptism.

Whilst one will probably not have a specific role as an ordained minister at work, a vocation that allows one's calling as an ordained minister to be shaped by and within the work environment is a different matter. What form that takes will depend on the context.[40] It also has to be said that the traditional role(s) of ordained ministry in the Church are changing, in light of a rediscovery of the place of the laity within the life of the Church as a whole. The value of the experience and expertise of MSE in this development is a resource that is yet to be adequately appreciated.

Here the model of "servant" is often to the fore in MSE.[41] This is of significance in relation to what Douglas Davies calls *"liminality"* and *"communitas"*.[42] *Liminality* refers to times and occasions in life where people find themselves in a moment of transition, as at a threshold, (whether in sorrow or joy). And *communitas* is the fellowship amongst others who know or enter into this experience. While *liminality* is not to be confused with marginality, which has to do with being at the edge of a significant group, it may be possible to be a "liminal witness" in a sort of mediatorial way between different groups.[43] The experience and expertise of the MSE may come to the fore in such circumstances as these, as representative person both so far as the Church is concerned but also within the embedded context of the workplace as a colleague. Davies surmises that the eucharistic significance of fellowship (*koinōnia*) may become so internalized in the MSE that (s)he is able to take it into the work setting and recognize *liminality* and *communitas* as these occur.

If this is true, then it gives a deep coherence to this kind of ministry in its representative meaning. It is one that informs the whole life experience of the MSE. And as improvisation it is not to be reduced to a matter of balancing roles. We have to avoid making ministry so far as MSE is concerned too narrowly focused on parochial models of thinking. The living link between Church and work cannot and should not mean that the traditional roles of authorized ministry in Church become the touchstone of the MSE's ministry in the workplace. Anthea Mitchell (MSE and hair stylist) describes her ministry thus:

It is evident that there is ministry in this, building relationships
with people . . . the highs, the lows. The idea is that I am a vicar
and a hairdresser at the same time, not sometimes a vicar and
sometimes a hairdresser. So the main area of my ministry is my
workplace; this is where I do most of my work. I think the two go
absolutely well together. As a hairdresser you build relationships
with people. They learn to trust you and you have really deep
conversations, maybe not about God actually but often about
spiritual matters."[44]

As Rowan Williams reminds us, "there is *no* one way of being a priest"
(italics his).[45] So it emerges that in comparison with the parish minister,
MSE is inherently more diffuse in its expression, something to be both
expected and welcomed.

From the foregoing, it can be seen that self-supporting ministry
where a minister is engaged one way or another with the world of work
can structure this relationship in various ways. Historically speaking,
discussions and debates in the Church on the emergence of MSE have
directly or indirectly touched on all of the key themes of discipleship,
vocation, and the relationship between Church and society. And they
continue to feature in the treasury of understanding that MSEs draw upon
to explain and explore the characteristics of this kind of ministry. From
the extended historical study of self-supporting ministry undertaken by
Patrick Vaughan we may note how self-supporting ministers have:

1. Made a contribution, by working for a living, to the affirmation
    of the connection between God and creation, the spiritual and
    the material. Clearly, this has found expression in different ways
    and at different times as culture and society itself have raised
    questions about how these are connected. The arguments with
    Gnosticism in the early centuries over divinity and materiality
    are not the same as the arguments in our time over sacred and
    secular. But even so, the presence of self-supporting ministers has
    borne a small but not insignificant contributory witness to belief
    in the Incarnation. Other principal reasons were to set a good
    example (in thrift and self-reliance), to be able to offer pastoral

care to others in appropriate settings, and to bear witness to faith in Christ.

2. Been something of a living reminder of the importance of non-theological matters in theological discussion. After all, not all such clergy worked for a living for theological or missionary-minded purposes, but for expediency e.g. financial reasons. These financial reasons included the fact occasionally that the Church was not wealthy enough to support them. This kind of ministry could be practised by default, as it were, as well as by choice. It might also be by Church expectation, as a positive expectation that clergy should do this.

3. Explained their ministry not necessarily on the basis of one single reason but occasionally (e.g. Paul, see the Excursus) for a number of reasons. Thus not only is this ministry diverse in its forms, but the rationale for it can also be varied. It is also worth noting how Paul's explanation of his tentmaking ministry strengthens the affirmation of work as an important and integral part of our calling, not a distraction from it (as in the Graeco-Roman view).

As the western and eastern Churches divided, clergy occupations in the west emerged from roles and responsibilities in teaching and administration come by in the later stages of the Roman Empire and into the Elizabethan Settlement (adding to existing occupations such as farmers and smallholders). In the eastern Church, where bishops were drawn from the monastic orders, clergy continued in much the same way, often supporting themselves in local contexts. The diversity attaching to self-supporting clergy in their work and their motives within differing cultural and social settings generally suggests an adaptive and pragmatic theologizing.[46]

CHAPTER 2

The Characteristics of a Busking Style

Those who would enquire into the significance of ministry in secular employment will find themselves inexorably drawn into an array of significant and deep questions. This itself is interesting in that ministry in secular employment not only centres on an exploration of a particular expression of ordained ministry (which of course it is), but also leads to some fundamental questions about ministry itself. Questions soon arise, as we shall see, about vocation (calling), discipleship, ordination and (not least) core values of humanity that enable the Church to engage with society generally.[47] In fact, theological reflection on MSE lies in the interrelationship of all these things working together and interacting with each other. While this study cannot undertake an examination of these in their own right, it signals afresh at the outset the breadth of themes that MSE addresses.

A standard dictionary defines (and thus literalizes) busking as "to play music in a public place for voluntary donations". Ironically, self-supporting ministry struggles to escape the discussion about finance. The origins of SSM as non-stipendiary ministry defined it, until it managed to change to the (even now not wholly satisfactory) term of self-supporting ministry, to avoid beginning with a negative (non-) and to escape from invidious comparison with those in receipt of a stipend. Most people outside the Church, and some within it, assume that a stipendiary minister is paid for their ministry rather than receiving an income to enable them to exercise it (Galatians 6:6 is likely the earliest reference to this[48]).

But let us face the underlying question squarely. Busking could be said to be unsuitable as a description of ministry, since any residual metaphorical meaning has been overtaken by the literal presence of those who busk in order to earn a living. It sits uneasily with ministry, which amongst other things is about care for others (particularly the poor) and concern for the world. That some in the history of the Church have busked to support themselves for the sake of their ministry is largely now forgotten. Nevertheless, in response to an implicit value judgement arising from the received notion of busking—doing something for oneself as distinct from doing something for others—the idea is actually more varied and more nuanced.

For one thing, not all who busk do it for themselves but for charitable causes. Moreover, as the trumpeter John Barker puts it, "Some professional musicians busk as a way of extending their musical practice and performance experience in a variety of contexts".[49] More recently busking as a metaphor has come into use as a means of communication in learning and teaching approaches in maths and science.[50] And from a linguistic perspective metaphors are not to be constrained by literal interpretation. Deliteralization is a semantic process by which a word appearing in a given context, and usually understood in its literal sense, may receive or may recover a non-literal meaning in a new or renewed referent.[51] The meaning of metaphors is essentially a matter of appropriateness.[52]

We suggest that there is enough scope for busking to remain a valid metaphor for improvisation, with something about it of marginality, change and liminality reflective of contemporary society. Given the association between busking and performance two illustrations may not be out of place. In Homeric forms of oral poetry, there was very likely improvisation present. This suggests that these poems worked not simply with standard formulaic phrases, but with a range of descriptions which allowed the bard to improvise spontaneously according to the space available within the line of the metre.[53]

Similarly in music, improvisation is following the implications of a shape, seeing the melody as a breadth, a horizon, a direction of a rhythm. Busking as an image also engages our senses one way or another (as do the Gospels) in the incarnational nature of Christian faith.[54] It is this that characterizes MSEs, who inhabit the metaphor in shaping their ministry. To put it succinctly, for MSE, busking as a creative description of ministry maps from source to target in the extempore characteristic of self-support, in distinction from the literalizing of busking as a means of income for self-support.

Busking is an intentional openness to the presence of God through being immersed in the daily life of the world as a sign of the Gospel present there, and to encourage believers in, and share with them, their life in the world. The verbs "to come" and "to go" are significant in this regard. Most stipendiary and parish-focused self-supporting ministers (who make up the majority of SSMs) will use the verb "to come" in terms of the invitation to Church (in its worship and pastoral resources). But in truth the large majority of a congregation speaks rather of going to Church, and of coming back out into the world that they inhabit. Ministers in secular employment are those who are vocationally informed by the verb "to go"—responding to the call of God (Isaiah 6:8: "Whom shall we send and who will go for us?") in terms of how, almost like balladeers, they construct their understanding of the world *in situ* as the locus of their ministry. Ministry in secular employment has a fundamental characteristic of improvisation. Perhaps this belongs to all forms of representative ministry, but none more than MSE.

Accordingly, we may ponder a notable and apposite statement, drawing on the metaphor of busking, by Ken Mason in his book *Priesthood and Society*:

> . . . the eucharist has to provide the theological foundation for ideas about the Church's priesthood. So far as the Church had any theory of its own priesthood, it was one that stressed the sacrificial character of the eucharist and the priestly character within the church of the local bishop, at whose hands and through whose prayer the eucharistic offering was made. Let us rather take note first of its unsettling, vertiginous character, if it is to be made part of the social theory of the Church's life. For to take a priesthood understood in that way and to make it the sacral priesthood of all society is like a king taking a busking comedian and making him, not merely the jester, but the chief protocol in his court. In a court of that kind, managed by such a person, etiquette and decorum will suddenly seem to be stretched very thin, dependent as they are on irony as much as good will.

A social culture that elects to make the eucharist its cultic centre is one that must become less and less secure in itself the nearer it gets to that centre, because a eucharistic culture is one that mocks a man's desire to create his own security . . . Even within the most complacent presentation of the eucharist the discomfort of Christ's redemptive work remains, challenging our illusion of peace but healing our distress. Underneath the new robes, the ragged motley of the busker remains visible.[55]

Priesthood in its context in the world[56] is presented in a striking way as a busking jester, akin to Paul's description of being a fool for the sake of Christ (1 Corinthians 4:10).[57] MSE in all its variety as an "edge" ministry bears witnesses to this. Let us then explore some of the characteristics of busking as a metaphor for MSE, which in their own way resonate with this image. While there may be many, we will suggest four that are significant, and feature in MSE stories. They are context, spontaneity, provisionality and perseverance.

Busking has an immediate affinity with context, of being simultaneously at the edge and on the spot. It is at the edge from which to impinge on people's consciousness in being (literally) sufficiently attractive to elicit a response. And it is on the spot in being sufficiently present to hold, even fleetingly, the potentiality "of the moment". A key theological characteristic in light of this will be the recollection that God is always a God of place. God meets us in specifics. But holy ground will not necessarily be in the temple—a bush on fire was Moses' vision of God. In Jesus, the Word made flesh, our meeting with others (in person or online) is always holy ground. Bryony Franklin (MSE and hospital pharmacist) says about the journey with COVID-19: "I feel that the most important thing I can offer to others is just listening."[58] Surely Peter Baelz is right in his claim that:

There is a hidden and anonymous church in the world wherever and whenever there is a response to the challenges of life with care and love; and the world is to be found in the Church wherever the Church conducts its affairs in the public sphere as one institution among many . . . Both are expressions of the way in which God rules his creation.[59]

Spontaneity is also a hallmark of busking. While busking may not always be noted for a sensitive awareness of context, it can often attract an appreciative response. Paul's adaptive claim "to be all things to all people" (in themes such as grace, freedom and justification by faith) had a kind of responsiveness in improvisation, as he sought to enable the arrival of God's kingdom in celebration, penitence, renewal and hope. In this, he responded to circumstance and opportunity. Likewise, the MSE will gradually pick up a sort of sixth sense in a ministry attuned to its context. Robert Fox (MSE and tax adviser working for HMRC) says (during COVID-19):

> In working online from home there have been unexpected advantages in speaking to and supporting colleagues. The "water cooler" moments have gone, but it is now easier to initiate the "how are you?" questions by messaging folk. In the office when someone wanted a private conversation it was often difficult to do this without others noticing, but when we are all at home it is much simpler, and I have found that many colleagues are actually more willing to chat about personal aspects of their lives . . . Overall, ministry in the workplace does not feel very different. In some ways it looks different, with virtual now dominant over the physical presence, but it is just as personal, just as relevant.[60]

At the very least (to borrow a phrase from the worker priest movement, which though distinctive from MSE has resonances with it), it is about "being there" and seeing what comes up. Its hallmarks are pragmatism and prayer. Peter Baelz in *Ministers of the Kingdom* notes that "the world in which Christians are called to witness to God is, objectively speaking, an ambiguous world, a mixture of potentialities for good and evil, and consequently open to more than one interpretation"; and that in light of being a created world imbued with predicament "the processes of creation are hazardous, even when the creator is God".[61]

This being so, it is obvious that on the one hand there is goodwill and creativity abroad in humankind even where a specific belief in God may be absent, and on the other hand Christian faith is not a package which can simply be applied to correct what is deficient, and above all, that Incarnation is the becoming of God's redemptive creativity in our world.[62] The incarnational basis of the Church gives a sacramental meaning to being present and participative in the world.

Busking is also marked by provisionality. It is a transient activity, making the most of the moment and of what is "in the moment". Here we encounter the provisionality of the Church, both in having wider boundaries than it thinks it might have, and also in having to work in ways that are open to change.[63] An incarnational model of the Church and a pilgrim metaphor for the Church may at times exist in tension. A pilgrim metaphor for the Church can suggest a passing through the world without necessarily engaging with it. Incarnation delivers presence, and pilgrimage delivers movement.

But as to provisionality, presence has to be about what questions the *status quo* through seeking its transformation, and pilgrimage has to be about serving that is not done merely in the passing and would leave the Church itself untouched. A theology of MSE has to address the provisionality of all things, which belongs to the very nature of work, and the signs of God's kingdom that reflect the glory of God amid the inherent flux of creation and human endeavour. Phil Aspinall (MSE and Process Risk Consultant) says succinctly and prophetically of the present work environment: "Always insecurity!"[64] A busking approach will seek to take this seriously in a ministry that is present within the world of work amid its inherent ambiguities and potentialities.

Again, this improvisation takes perseverance. It is an out there, on the streets kind of public ministry that is far from the known and recognized parameters of the Church, open to criticisms as well as compliments; and (not infrequently) to simply being ignored, knowing at first hand (and having to bear) the irrelevance of the Church for so many people. In the New Testament this characteristic of the Spirit is described as steadfastness ("*hupomoné*"), constancy sustained by expectation. (The number of occurrences, thirty-two, of "*hupomoné*" in the New Testament is notable.) It is this, perhaps, that is the best appreciation of the meaning of "being there". A sense of struggle, patience and even failure, in the experience of ministry at work is something that is there in the writings of the worker priests and MSE stories.[65] Wendy White (MSE and working in the charity sector) reflects on the experience of furlough during the COVID-19 pandemic:

> We are brought up, in the main, to regard filling each minute with meaningful activity—whether we have "inherited" Kipling's unforgiving minute or simply heard the call for the labourers to come to the field because the harvest is plentiful. If we are lucky, we may also have heard the need for time and prayer and even putting a short retreat into the diary. Furlough has banished all this . . . It is not that I have sat silent and thoughtful for three months, furloughed from a job that creates space and support for cancer patients, I had other skills that could be used indirectly—I have been making scrubs and masks among other things, I could act as chaplain to those still working and simply listen. But it came as a shock to find that unpredicted quiet time and space was unnerving . . . I am back from enforced stillness now, just, and beginning to see it as a blessing . . . I am praying that the relinquishing of control and the sense of assenting to an absence rather than demanding a presence (Charles Williams) can inform how I move forward.[66]

Such perspectives as these help to shape and inform the theology and practice of ministry in secular employment. They do not imply the casualization of ministry, as though it were individualistic or lacking in accountability. On the contrary, they shape the narrative of MSE in a coherent and responsible way. As we shall see later on, these four characteristics of busking also inform four aspects of MSE spirituality.[67]

This "busking" dynamic arguably underlies the ministry of Jesus himself, no less. This is particularly worth noting in relation to the contrast sometimes made (and overdrawn, see the Excursus) between a supported style of mission on the part of Jesus and the disciples on the one hand, and the self-supporting ministry of Paul and others on the other hand.

Traditionally, the Church in its ordination liturgy reflects the call of the first disciples as a turning away from the occupations and securities of the world for the sake of the mission of the kingdom of God. (Perhaps this is the origin of the occasional description of ordained ministry as a "going into the Church".) The *fisher-folk* whom Jesus met became *fishers of folk*, an undoubted pun in Jesus' words to Peter, James and John in leaving their nets and entering upon the mission of the kingdom of God. Jesus and the disciples were themselves supported by others—entertained and fed by sympathizers or interested people, and financially maintained (Luke 8:3; cf. 23:49,55). And Jesus in sending out his disciples on mission invited them to rely on the support of others.

Even so, commensurate with the calling of Jesus to go into the world the style of MSEs who intentionally shape their ministry within the secular reflects its own full measure of risk and challenge. The ironic question which lies at the heart of John's Gospel, "Can anything good come out of Nazareth?" is answered with an invitation, one that unites imagination with discovery: "Come and see" (1:46). We may accordingly map the characteristics of busking to Jesus' ministry:

1. The context of Jesus' message was quite different from our own. Not only was that world different socially, culturally and technologically, it was a religiously imbued society. There was a ready audience for his ministry and his message. Nevertheless, it worked both "from the edge" and "at the margin" of people's expectations. Clearly the locations of his mission were consonant with a peripatetic ministry, but Jesus chose his own ground so that where he placed himself enabled or contributed to his preaching, or on occasion conveyed symbolic meaning. Even in the robust encounter with the Syrophoenician woman in Mark 7:24–30 Jesus had chosen to go to that region and to be there.

2. Jesus' style was characterized by spontaneity, carefully argued but with a certain open style. Those who responded to his message were by and large the non-aligned "people of the land" who also noted its difference from much of the teaching of the day. The religious authorities certainly did, as it came gradually to their notice in questioning Jesus' pedigree and authority. Whilst there

is a coherence and consistency about all that he said and did, there is also a creativity about the different ways in which his ministry was inherently bound up with his message. The kingdom takes shape in its strength and vulnerability within the developing and changing structure of his own life and in its relationship to others, as suggested by the parable of the sower (Mark 4:3–8). It was not simply the interpretation of truth in a measured, discursive way, though he was capable of that. His teaching had a pithy, imagistic realism about it. Certainly the parables challenge the hearer to see truth in a new light, and to accept and absorb its truth in their own way within their context.

3. Jesus' message in its eschatological urgency sounded a note of provisionality to everything. This includes the ways in which the particular group of his followers also had porous boundaries, one in which outsiders as well as insiders, and sometimes they more truly, could grasp the reality of the kingdom (cf. Mark 9:38ff.).

4. Certainly Jesus' ministry took perseverance—there are observations in the Gospels about his own struggle in the mission of the kingdom e.g. in the face of unbelief, the assessment of his family, his "setting his face" towards Jerusalem, the vacillation of his disciples and their desertion, Gethsemane, betrayal and indeed the cry of dereliction from the Cross. Although the Church looking back affirmed the achievement of God's purpose throughout his ministry, it is surely the case that Jesus reckoned with the probability of rejection.

Overall, we might say that Jesus' ministry takes its chance. It is one that also established a trajectory by which signs of the presence of God were not necessarily those that were traditionally obtained within organized religion, either in his own day or subsequently within the Church. We have moved in this discussion from highlighting some characteristics of busking to finding them in Jesus' ministry. But turning that around, we can find the characteristics because this was his style anyway. Some of the same characteristics appear in Paul's tentmaking ministry, and which confirm the theological rationale that enabled Paul to depart occasionally from the traditional style of an apostle dependent on the funding of the church. Indeed Paul, in 1 Corinthians 9, improvises with how the message of the gospel is presented through the ministry of the gospel. This would further reflect the busking image of Christ's priesthood in the Church's discipleship, as Ken Mason has suggested. If that is found specifically in the context of ministry in secular employment it is valid. Perhaps enough has been noted to show how an understanding of MSE is about far more than purely procedural questions in tracing back forms of ministry to whether they were supported or self-supporting. There is something fundamental in theological vision that connects MSE to the path of the gospel, one that runs deeper than questions about forms of maintenance, interesting though these are.

MSEs learn to improvise, become buskers perforce, as they express through their work the narrative of the kingdom. Keith Tripp (MSE and Business Development Director of St John's College Nottingham) says: "We do not know what we will encounter on a day to day basis, so we need to be prepared with the Holy Spirit to adapt and improvise accordingly."[68] Rowan Williams reflects on how God (in Jesus) is "inside" human motivation and how this gives to Jesus' own struggles "a sense of the precariousness of goodness, love and fidelity", which precariousness is the very way in which God is always present and meeting us.[69] MSE is not extrapolating from some other sort of ministry, particularly the familiar stipendiary model. It is an authentic form of ministry in its own right, one that deserves better training and resourcing by the Church than it currently receives.

CHAPTER 3

Busking the Gospel: Dimensions

The improvisatory nature of this ministry invites us to a theology that has a certain panoramic quality to it. This interweaving ministry gives the MSE the opportunity, challenge and privilege of bringing faith and work together on behalf of the Church in its life in and for the world.[70] It is of course the gospel that holds the motivation and the vision for discipleship and ministry. There are four Gospels. It is not so much that there is a core gospel, which is given variety in four ways. Rather there are four different "takes" on the mystery of Jesus Christ as the glory of God in human form in the midst of the created order—the living embodiment of all the creation-rooted meaning of the tabernacle. The gospel conveys the inherent possibility of developing a variety of theological perspectives on the kingdom of God and the Incarnation (on which see further below).

Accordingly, a theology of MSE also does not lie in any one thing but in four things, we may call them dimensions, working together in a sort of inter-animation. These are discipleship, ministry, human flourishing and sociality. It is these four working together in a creative interaction that contribute to an adequate understanding of MSE. The living out of the gospel in the vision of MSE is, one way or another, about these four dimensions being improvised or busked in creative ways.

Of course everyone has to do this in their own way. This is a chart rather than a map, a sketch and not a blueprint, guidelines (as for an actor) or notes to create a harmony (as for a musician). To neglect or to emphasize any one at the expense of the others will bring distortion. These four dimensions are intrinsic to the challenge that MSE presents. For example, if MSE has been mistakenly accused of undermining the ministry of the laity, then that raises the question of what the discipleship and ministry of the whole people of God is, and the meaning of ordination. Again,

MSE embedded in a working life focuses on the meaning and purpose of human creativity, of vocation as human fulfilment. And because this is a ministry at the margins of the Church but in a close engagement with society it raises questions of what the roots of a healthy society are. We can set out the dimensions thus:

- The discipleship of all God's people
- The significance of ministry
- Human flourishing
- Sociality

Giving these dimensions or parameters a shape expressed as breadth, length, height and depth[71] we might say:

1. Breadth: Discipleship has to do with the breadth of the Church, if it is to live up to the claim to be that part of creation wherein its fulfilment in Christ is glimpsed.
2. Length: Tradition and length go together in terms of the story of the gospel, with the particular responsibility of ordained ministry to sign, nurture, affirm and explore its meaning.
3. Height: Our flourishing and our creativity combine in a way that has to do with height (aspiration) in the fulfilment of God's will "as in heaven so on earth".
4. Depth: The challenge of wrestling with contextual questions is about depth, in engaging with what makes for the wellbeing of society in community.

Bringing this together as a chart, we might present it thus:

**The discipleship of
all God's people**
The Church as that part of
God's world in which the
divine love in Christ is already
acknowledged and celebrated.
(Breadth)

Human flourishing
What does the sense of calling
in Christ "to be a human
being fully alive" mean?
(Height)

———————   **Identity in Christ**   ———————

Ministry
Signing and enabling others
to hold the story-tradition
and vision of the Gospel.
(Length)

Sociality
What does it mean to claim
e.g. "The Lord is here" in
nurturing community?
(Depth)

Interestingly, the interrogatives attach themselves to the dimensions of flourishing and sociality. Significantly we should be allowing these to interrogate the indicatives of discipleship and ministry rather than these being simply "fields of application" of what we think discipleship and ministry mean. It would seem that in a profound way MSE is a contribution to the mission of the Church as a whole, simply because everywhere is holy ground. The Church must be for the world as God is God of all the world.

An adequate theology of MSE requires the interaction of these four dimensions. How that is done and what will emerge will be the creativity of an individual's understanding of their ministry. Nor do they have to be present in equal measure, as if it were simply sounding four notes with equal loudness with no sense of musicality, or as if it were reciting a line of poetry with no intonation or sense of rhythm. These are the notes with which to improvise, to build the line of a melody, to improvise on themes as though telling a story. It is the given of a ministry of the gospel with which, after a manner of speaking, to "wing it". David Jasper reminds us of how "faith in conversation with art and poetry discerns the beauty that resides in the commonplace and everyday, the world in a grain of sand, the ever new glories of both the natural and the sublime".[72]

That these four dimensions should interact with each other is based on the premise that who we are in Christ is relational, rooted in the understanding of God as the One who calls. Christopher Cocksworth and Rosalind Brown in their book *Being a Priest Today* affirm this, and it is worth quoting at length what they say:

> Christian identity is fundamentally relational. It is a called identity, a vocational identity. This calling into Christ precedes what we do for Christ, and even how we live for Christ, though at the same time it predetermines our doing and being as Christians . . . Function is a modern mechanical concept, concerned with productivity. Ontology is a Greek philosophical concept, concerned with questions of being or existence. Both may betray a predilection for power—power that comes from effective control over sources and systems, or power that comes from a permanent, guaranteed existence in the scheme of things. But the only power that Jesus offers his disciples is the power of love . . . This dynamic, energetic, relational vitality is the sap of Christian life that propels us into Christian ministry as we live from the life of Christ into which we have been called. All that we are in Christ and all that we do for Christ arise from a vocation, a calling into a certain sort of relation to him—a relationship of extraordinary grace.[73]

In light of this, which helpfully roots ordination securely in a context that transcends the oft-quoted polarities of doing and being, we can see how the central focus of "identity in Christ" is the basis of holding the dimensions of the discipleship of all God's people, ordination, human flourishing and sociality together. The four exist in relation to each other, and are themselves a partnership rather than a hierarchy. So now let us turn to a consideration of these dimensions, and how they shape the improvisatory nature of MSE.

The discipleship of all God's people

Whilst it has become almost commonplace to speak of the ministry of all God's people (perhaps by that meaning the ministry of the laity so as to counter an idea of clerisy), it might actually be preferable to speak of the discipleship of the people of God, and ministry as that which (for clarity at least) belongs to particular responsibilities within and on behalf of the Church.[74] The ministry of the laity is probably too big a jump in any theology of the Church rooted in the understanding of baptism because it omits (almost by default) the central idea that faith is rooted primarily in discipleship. The primary vocation of the Church is not to ministry but to discipleship. Ministry is more specifically about the authorized office and work of a person within and on behalf of the Church (and correspondingly the question of accountability). Very likely the ministry of the Church is in fact the offering (a priestly task) of its discipleship in Christ to God. Paul hints as much in Romans 12:1 in the idea of presenting "your bodies as a living sacrifice, holy and acceptable to God which is your spiritual worship".[75]

The Church is called to be a sign and instrument of the kingdom of God reaching out to the world. Its mission is proclamation, service and community. It reflects the one high priesthood of Christ. When those about to be ordained are presented to the congregation, the people are asked, "Will you uphold them in their ministry?" and they reply, "We will." As the whole people of God speak this, they are in effect reflecting something of themselves about their own discipleship. MSEs affirm this in a particular way. That is to say, it is not only the function of the ordained to encourage the people of God in their life and witness in the world but to share in what is the necessary presence of the Church in the world. MSEs sign the significance of discipleship that is the ministry of the whole people of God, equipping and encouraging them to be confident and articulate believers in the world, and to help them to reflect more deeply about the world and God's purpose being worked out.

It is perhaps worth pointing to a statement on *The Mission and Ministry of the Whole Church*.[76] To be welcomed is the affirmation that mission is "the whole Church proclaiming the whole Christ to the whole world", together with the appreciation of the public role of the Church in the affairs of the world.[77] That said, in its conclusion " . . . the Church is commissioned by Christ primarily to carry out a ministry of word, sacrament and pastoral care", valid though this is, one cannot but feel a certain loss of nerve in the face of so much potential for a theological grounding for mission promised in the earlier statements.

Above all discipleship is helping people to see and to find themselves in whatever is discovered, celebrated and offered by the presence of Christ through the Church. This means that it is for clergy to enable the Church to be a wide enough space for the public to be engaged with it. This is surely a key contributing aim for MSE. It is about what one is present to, a self-involvement in the sense of what matters in faith and living—not just as a ministry at work but how "being set amongst others" raises questions and brings opportunities relating to where and how one is present to life's meaning, to creativity and human purposing, all of which are central to the gospel.

Ministry

Michael Ramsey remarked:

> If you want to know what clergy are for, do not start with pragmatic considerations, the jobs you would like clergy to do in running things or providing "leadership"; start with the picture of an assembly that . . . draws you towards a contemplative understanding of the act of God in Cross and Resurrection, and in the eternal love by which God is God.[78]

It is very clear that discussion about the emergence of SSM in modern times has centred on the meanings of both Church and ordination.[79] It is also worth pointing out that the understanding of ordination has changed over time if we compare for example the Book of Common Prayer with Common Worship. For one thing, the description has lengthened, and in light of the emergence of a variety of authorized ministries in the Church there is a much stronger note of sharing and collaboration. As already stated, however, it is probably preferable for clarity to speak of the discipleship of the whole people of God, and to use the term "ministry" for particular offices and responsibilities within and on behalf of the Church.[80]

Ordination belongs within the whole priestly ministry of the Church in its indwelling in Christ. Perhaps we might express it thus: if the ministry of the Church is to offer its discipleship in the service of Christ, the discipleship of the ordained ministry is to sign what this means, for and on behalf of the Church in its witness to Christ. Vincent Donovan remarks:

> The "priesthood of all believers" has often been used as an empty slogan by Catholics and Protestants alike. Catholics do not want to apply the priesthood to all believers, to the laos, the people of God, the laity. Protestants often use the phrase in a negative way. By stressing the second part of the phrase, they in fact deny the first part, or at least put a brake on the deepest sacramental, sacrificial and incarnational meaning of the priesthood of Jesus Christ. If only the Catholic meaning of priesthood could come to live with the Protestant meaning of faithful in the Church, we might yet arrive at a new understanding of the power and glory of Christianity.[81]

MSE takes us in some ways to the heart of the discussion of what ordination is (within Anglicanism).[82] It raises questions (as we have seen) about whether the presence of the laity is being devalued, and also what ordination means in relation to one's work.[83] The meaning of MSE however, remains just what priesthood is, namely to exemplify to the whole Church its priestly calling to imitate Christ "to enact the presence and life of Christ in the world". And if we ask what this means it corresponds to the characteristic of the Church as that part of God's world in which the divine love in Christ is already acknowledged and celebrated.[84]

In reflecting (from John Mantle's book) on WP and MSE it is evident from the narrative that, as a matter of regret, MSEs did not at first really engage with WPs. And certainly, there are differences e.g. at the level of vocation: i) WPs were trained priests who embraced the world of work as distinct from MSE, which is about training people who will remain in their work; and ii) the WP model was addressed to working class culture and jobs. There was a more radical vision from the outset. Nevertheless, it is important to note that a) WPs did influence the emergence of NSM/MSE e.g. English WPs did relate to Church and its congregational life;[85] and b) (significantly) WPs also struggled to articulate a theology.[86]

Here a number of things are worth saying.

First, the MSE's understanding of ordination will be influenced by a contextual understanding of Church and society, and shaped by the challenge and experience of what it means to express ministry in the workplace.

Second, MSEs will be disposed to express their ministry in ways that are recognizable within the framework of ordained ministry informed by the Church at large:

> How you think about theology . . . actually depends in the long run on how you are thinking about the Church in the first place . . . What we say about theology depends on our theology of the Church. However, I have in mind not so much some sort of "given" doctrine of the Church but rather the underlying imperfectly voiced assumptions as to the sort of thing the Church is—which in turn reflect the underlying assumptions as to the nature of what (if anything) is done for us in the events of Jesus' life and death.[87]

From the study of MSE stories collected in the volume *Ministers of the Kingdom*, these express themselves in ministry exercised within the work setting in eight forms: interpreter, teacher, counsellor, confessor, comforter, reconciler, intercessor, nucleus (for Christian groups).[88] One that is more implicit than explicit is prophet, it being pointed out that this is something of a difference between MSE and a chaplain/sector ministry model. It may be that a "detached within" stance of the chaplain is more able to voice a prophetic comment where relevant.

However, one wonders just what "prophetic" means here, if it is more than "a word in season", and relies too much on a distinction (in its biblical roots) between prophecy and wisdom. MSEs will know more than most how unhelpful an ill-judged comment can be in context. Very likely in the stories recorded there are instances that could be considered "prophetic" without being labelled as such. It just depends on what one is conditioned to recognize. But arguably the form of celebrant is not absent here, even if by and large it is rooted in the life of the Church that exists in gathered rather than dispersed mode.

There is actually a sort of parallel here between the MSE and a parish priest. Just as the latter will structure the relationship between congregation and parish loosely, finding ministry taking shape in a parish whilst rooted in the congregation, so the MSE will see what emerges in "going with the grain" of the workplace.

Third, MSEs universally recognize and affirm that theirs is a public ministry, in keeping with the Church's understanding of ordained ministry generally. And, importantly, they note that it is received as such. The difficulty for MSE can be a sort of projection (though not necessarily false) by others of the Church as a self-contained religious sphere that is too wrapped up in itself. Or if their ministry is met, in turn, with a sort of religious functionalism that reckons things in terms of availability, and fails to appreciate the possibilities and realities for ministry in the dispersed life of the Church in the world, which can contribute so much to the enriching of the Church in gathered mode, then there is a job to be done in addressing caricatures on both sides of the coin. But actually there is an holistic heart to the whole significance of ordination, of a "to-ing and fro-ing" in the rhythm of the Church in its presence in the world in as seamless a way as possible, even if it needs an understanding of work all round to see it, and mutual effort all round to work at it.

We have already noted that the Church's understanding of ordination is something that is not static but reflects its relationship with the world. It cannot be otherwise if ordination is a public office of the Church. MSEs therefore have to work at how their experience of ministry in the world articulates with the received statements according to which they were ordained.[89] But for that to happen MSEs require to be a constant and influential presence within the Church.[90]

Very likely all this sets an understanding of ordination within the work of the Spirit, rather than the frequent Christological context of apostolic succession. It is really the Church in its whole being that inherits this responsibility. The Church's quest for, and affirmation of unity, vitality and order as gifts of the Spirit are themselves manifestations of the kingdom—bringing creation into unity with God, and the celebration of God in the creativity of life in ways that are both peaceable and purposeful. Placing the understanding of ordination under a doctrine of the Holy Spirit means that the Church has to recognize that its understanding of ordination has changed over time as it engages with the world, and (just as importantly) has itself had to be responsive to change in the world.

There are generic descriptions of ordained ministry. But this ministry does not exist in a vacuum, just as the Church does not exist in a vacuum. Understandings of ordination are rightly moulded by a wide understanding of the discipleship of believers on the one hand in a calling to faith whose hallmark should be our humanity and creativity in Christ, and on the other hand should be responsive to the changing world where God is always actively present. A fundamental value of ordained ministry is discovery, which improvises with the interaction of these perspectives.[91]

MSE also raises a number of important questions about the relationship between vocation and role. If an MSE is not functioning in an authorized pastoral role in their work what does it mean to have a vocation to priesthood that is not (as it predominantly is in the Church) exercised through a role?

Very likely, MSE is a clue to an understanding of diaconate and priesthood that will want to avoid being reduced to roles, and not least roles understood in an ecclesiastical way.[92] The fundamental to ordained ministry is being human, and its purpose is to help others to be and to celebrate being human. To help to find and to make "depth connections" in life and for living, and to help others to do likewise, is the purpose of ordained ministry, even as Jesus said "I came that they might have life in all its fullness" (John 10:10). And that is for everyone and not just the Church. This is the secular meaning of sacraments, and this is the recognition that the secular is sacramental. Diaconal and priestly ministry in signing this are not taking something out of the Church into a different arena. They are envisaging the Church in the arena of the world as the creative sign that this is possible and necessary. As Deirdre

Palk (MSE deacon and consultant in health, safety and environmental management) says:

> Sacred and secular are united in my mind. I know that both church and world will try to separate them and I believe it is my highest calling to keep them together, to 'mind the gap' . . . The holy is in the ordinary. There is another world, but it is in this one.[93]

So the MSE enables the whole Church to affirm its presence in the world and focuses the realization to the world that the Church cares for it. The MSE might not celebrate sacraments in the workplace, but (s)he enables believers to live sacramentally, and (s)he points to the sacramental nature of God's love in Christ for the whole world. MSE contributes to an understanding of the ordained as the *animateur* of the people of God, at least by contributing a life at work as well as anywhere/everywhere else. In any case, and perhaps most important of all, there is the enduring importance of the hidden work of God in the kingdom that exists and complements the visible expressions of word and sacrament, as in the dimension of hiddenness in the parables of salt, mustard seed, treasure, pearl, and the faithful work that is involved in the uncovering and discovering of meaning.[94]

Human flourishing

If the Reformation rediscovered the notion of calling within the everyday, from the cloister to the occupations of daily life, in more recent times the association between fulfilment and work has centred upon creativity, in what motivates us, realizing our potential in that sense of what appeals (literally calls) to us to be or become. Work and its motivations reflect a sense of productivity—the effort put in so that the end outcome is serviceable or saleable. And work may also reflect what it affords the individual in terms of fulfilment and personal satisfaction. These are the objective and subjective views of work.[95] The objective view of work, whilst it can sustain motivation, may not lead to fulfilment if work itself is not satisfying. If work is boring or poorly paid or affected by working conditions, then it will not be fulfilling.

On the other hand, calling in relation to the subjective view of work is likely to be strong where there is an engagement that evokes both a commitment and an enthusiasm. When God saw all that he had made and said that it was good, there is something evocative in its very affirmation. This is another way by which we can appreciate how calling belongs in a primary sense to an understanding of God as the One who calls, indeed as the one who is always calling (1 Thessalonians 5:24, noting Paul's use of the present (continuous) participle in that verse). That being so, we should expect and look for all manner of ways of responding to God's call, whether that be overtly religious or not. That is to say, calling exists wherever people feel impelled to work for good, and to respond to whatever is inspiring them to discover and use gifts creatively.[96]

We must think on a broad and not a narrow canvas. The weakness in some modern perceptions of calling is how it can become narrowed in an individualistic way. Value becomes placed on contributions viewed atomistically, with the corresponding need to display to others, or even impress them with, one's own talents. This can also lead to an understanding of community that is primarily associational, a gathering either of the like-minded or the affirmation of a peer-approved group. In some ways, the rivalry over spiritual gifts at Corinth that Paul condemned has some of these features.

But for Paul, and classically in the Church, the giftedness of its members is not about a contribution of abilities for mutual recognition. Rather, it is the realization of what the one Spirit of God can do through our diversity to enable us to contribute to the life of faith that is shared by and expressed through the body. Another feature of working on a broad canvas is that our response to calling is always in some sense within the created order and not just the religious sphere. And if it is in the religious sphere it is recognizing that the Church is but that part of the world that acknowledges the divine purpose in Christ.

It is likely that one is called to serve God not exclusively within the Church but rather through the Church, since the Church is called to serve God in the world. It does not work for its own survival. It is this that will explain, in part, how the understanding of vocation to ordained ministry has changed over the centuries of the Church's existence, precisely because it is something that is contextual and has been shaped culturally. Significantly, also, if God's calling is rooted in relationship to the world, the call of Christ to which the Church responds is one that has an empathic engagement with other expressions of calling that can be varied and diffuse but which may share certain characteristics.[97] To a significant extent it is this that MSE taps into in the understanding of vocation.

Some other things are to be noted about calling. Firstly, answering to something that calls to us or summons us may be about what is uncovered or discovered. That is to say, a calling may be about the taking further of a gift in its awareness, or it may be a discovery (by self or others) of something we did not know. Very likely the discernment here will be different for different people and circumstances. Secondly, a sense of calling has to do with finding oneself, that sense of knowing what it is in Christ to be a human being fully alive. But this may be standing with Christ in the world where God has chosen to be, and that takes courage—a place of risk where there are no defensive walls, far (but for some free) from the protection of religiosity.

Calling is a wide-ranging expression of what matters, of what we consider to be significant and important. Some such markers of calling that bring together human wellbeing and Christian discipleship are these. Firstly, calling is about our place in the world, in the sense that the God who is calling is the Creator, and as likely as not our calling will have a sense of something expansive. Secondly it is about sociality—it is not a selfish thing, and therefore if it has to do with finding creativity it will, as the necessary context of discipleship, be about affirming our responsibility to and with others in the world around.[98] Thirdly, it will be about challenge—not a dignifying of the *status quo*—something that is again related to the kindred expression of discipleship as pilgrimage. And fourthly (following on from that), it is about hope, because calling is what beckons us towards the future. Whatever we may be being called to, there is the underlying fact that we are simply being called, beckoned towards discovery and possibility. In the end, calling is about a toast to life, as in the Jewish phrase *l'chaim*.

There are four clues, as that which is outward into creation, as that which makes for responsibility in fostering sociality, as that which is about pilgrimage, and as that which is about the future. These four allow for diversity in what might be contained within a sense of God as the One who is (always) calling, and the relationship between fulfilment and service as the opposite sides of a single coin. So, there is enough here for an MSE vocation to busk with, set within the experience of a working life.

The question of what is meant by fulfilment is particularly acute at the point of selection for ordained ministry. A candidate might affirm the importance of their work in articulating a vocation to ordained ministry. This sharpens the issue around the anticipated question, "What does ordained ministry mean for a work context in which a Christian vocation in discipleship is already being patiently expressed? The difficulty that a prospective MSE might meet in reply centres on the fact that the question is itself based upon the premise that ordination is being viewed here as a sort of value-added dimension to discipleship. If we further note that any vocation to authorized or representative ministry in the Church emerges from discipleship in any case, it is the lack of that acknowledgement in vocation discernment that can cause difficulty for (prospective) MSEs.

It has to be said that prospective MSEs are not sufficiently helped by the Church in articulating a sense of calling that is coherent and comprehensive. While selection for ordained ministry will be about more than the work context, it has to include it. What is a prospective MSE to say in articulating a sense of calling? The best way is to outline an understanding of ordained ministry that is holistic, that refuses to be compartmentalized, that resists language such as "part-time", and that shows how a work context is woven into a coherent vision for ministry that is, at heart, shaped by life and humanity. To do that is i) to ground calling in Incarnation, and ii) to be true to MSE that at heart is paradoxically more than the work context in a narrow sense precisely because it includes it. In other words, MSE is about a ministry that is being shaped by a sense of God's call throughout creation, and which will not come to an end when work, for whatever reason, comes to an end.

If this needs further theological underpinning, we might turn again to Michael Ramsey, who explores how the glory of God is disclosed in his created works (Psalm 19:1ff.; Romans 1:20).[99] From this fundamental claim that links calling to the affirmation of glory, we may glean the following insights:

1. God is known in creation and yet transcends it. God's act of creating is the overflowing of his glory that eternally lacks nothing. God and the cosmos are not mutually necessary for each other. But God gives God-self to the world in a continuous, donating, responsive regard towards it. (Some Jewish theology has argued for a measure of dependency of God upon his creation,[100] though Christian theology has tended to avoid this.) The Word in John 1:1 that echoes Genesis 1:1 is not a fiat/command independent from the establishment of a relationship, of what Simone Weil calls "a proportion, a harmony".[101] So we can rightly discern who God is through what God does, and the act of creation is simultaneously the establishing of a relationship with all that is created. Humankind is to have rule over creation, but on the basis that creation is itself related to God.[102] So this is not to be exploitation, something that breaches justice (though sadly this too often happens). Rather it is rooted in the generosity of God in all things, and which is the glory of God in all things (cf. Herbert's "A kinde of tune, which all things heare and fear" in his poem "Prayer".[103]) It is the Word that lies behind John 1:3ff., the Word that enlightens everyone, and therefore that which lies behind Jesus' words in Matthew 5:45, that God sends his rain on the just and the unjust alike. The glory of God is his generosity throughout all creation. "God owes it to his own infinite goodness to give to every creature good in all its fullness."[104] It is for the Church to bear witness to this, to live this, not to portion it out. It is the realization of this for which Paul longs in the redemption of the daughters and sons of God. It is this of which John speaks in saying that the world will know the disciples of Jesus, through the love of God which is revealed in their midst and which constitutes them as witnesses to it.

2. To glorify God is to rejoice in his works and our creativity in absolute dependence on the creator. There is always the danger of worshipping the creature in place of the creator. But equally there

is the possibility of the neglect of the testimony of God's glory in nature, humanity and history. The Johannine Jesus' exhortation to the disciples (15:8) reflects the commandment of God in creation to be fruitful and multiply. This is John's equivalent to Paul's claim that if anyone is in Christ they are a "new creation". But this new creation is the renewing of all creation, the reflection of God's glory in all that is, that all might receive (acknowledge, reflect) him (1:12–13).[105]

3. We have already noted how hope is a necessary element of the human condition. Traditionally the Church has associated eschatology with the hope of redemption, the resolution to the human predicament called (in Judaeo-Christian tradition) sin. The emergence of this hope in the Old Testament includes the whole of creation. Unfortunately, this eschatological hope became allied to the Classical idea of perfection. The hope of salvation tended thereby to view creation as flawed and in need of correction. The understanding of nature in the Western world has ever since shown a tension or ambivalence whether nature is naturally good,[106] or is flawed (due to some mysterious implication in human sin) and incomplete. If creation, however, is not bound to a (Greek) perfectionist view but is based instead on the vision of the goodness of God's work, this gives to human endeavour a fresh realization of engagement with God. Eschatology is surely nothing less than the affirmation of creation's affinity with its Creator. This is what lies behind the phrase of Tennyson, "I look at all things as they are, but through a kind of glory",[107] sensing how creation points to its Creator, which for the poet is both reality and hope. Paul in Romans 8:22 describes all creation as groaning (i.e. in labour pains, a positive birthing metaphor), conveying the longing of all things awaiting the fulfilment of the divine purpose revealed in Jesus. Thus Christian hope is necessary for the Church in the reminder of its own incompleteness in which it participates with the world generally, and is a sign thereby not to worship itself in being self-absorbed.

It is this that an MSE, together with all others in a local congregation can signify mutually through responding to the shared calling to affirm God's glory in the world. The contexts of Paul's mention of being a self-supporting apostle speak of the glory of God, his care for, and his companionship with others. He might not speak of work as a creative thing in and of itself. But we should not draw the conclusion that Paul did not value his work. That it was toilsome did not mean that it was unimportant. If others thought it was demeaning, according to the culture of the Graeco-Roman world of his day, Paul turned that to a theological lesson in discipleship in following the servant Christ.

Sociality

Participation in the world of work raises in its own way questions of social wellbeing, belief in a kind of "social glue" that undergirds society and invites consideration of kindred terms such as sociability and solidarity. Sociality can range from sharing a similar outlook to solidarity in a strong signification of belonging together, or even pulling together, not least under difficult circumstances. In reflecting on sociality, the MSE will have to negotiate different forms and types of participation as these shape and are shaped by the work environment.

It is also true that the context of ministry at work will also change in relation to other things that affect working life and community. Our modern world has become aware of the need to rediscover and affirm key elements that go towards the affirmation of a healthy society. Of course society changes and how community cohesion is shaped differs from age to age. The hierarchical way of working together by knowing one's place within a feudal structure is not ours in a flat, egalitarian, individualist world. And ours is an age that has been shaped and changed by the long-emerging struggle for human rights in its various expressions. Rabbi Jonathan Sacks notes how some virtues have emerged in a shift of culture, particularly tolerance from the seventeenth century onwards as a shift took place away from the previous bonds of class, religion and kinship.[108] Whatever the constants of the gospel (cf. Philippians 4:1ff.) they play out in social change.

Nevertheless, human beings have always sensed some underlying values that are essential to being human, and to living in ways that are societal. This is something found not only in education and social policy and planning, but also in a concern for patterns of work and business practice.[109] However it is described, there is what might be called a "social glue" that holds "the baseboard of human endeavour" together. Moreover, there is a growing recognition of certain things that belong to the substructure of society and the building blocks of community over which the market has no control, and which cannot be traded. It has to do with the bonds of humanity, respect (rights) and, perhaps, regard and even love. Paradoxically in the workplace, markets are not the only things that exist or even have a right to exist. This fundamental truth focuses the presence of the MSE as an ordained minister particularly in witness, encouragement, blessing and reconciling. James Handley (MSE and software developer) writes:

> I am an ordained minister in the Church of England and a professional software application developer. These two spheres do not have a lot of overlap. However computer source code does have a culture. Source code can be helpful and cooperative, easy to understand and maintain. Or it can be obstructive and difficult. It is nothing new to suggest that code can be good or bad. But if you see it as embodying a culture, then you could say it becomes a potential means of blessing or a means of curse; easy to work with, or difficult and obstructive. A principal way that I interact with my colleagues (and indeed our customers) is through the code I write. If I write code badly this causes pain for my immediate colleagues, as well as those to come. On the other hand if I write code well this can be a source of blessing to my colleagues. They can pick up what I have written, easily understand what it is doing and why I wrote it that way, and make whatever modifications they may need to. Might it be that one of the ways I can exercise a priestly ministry at work is by writing code that is a means of blessing—by that I mean my work bringing pleasure to others; beautiful, well crafted and elegant code that is a blessing to work with. But even "cursed" code can

usually be "saved". It can be re-written or refactored into blessed
code—and might this in turn be a picture of reconciliation and
redemption? If we are working to create a blessed environment
within which to be joyful and fruitful in our labour, that is
something of the kingdom of God, surely. Let us be clear that
every Christian, whether employed or not, whether ordained or
not should be asking themselves these sorts of questions. Another
way of expressing it might be, "In what way am I participating
in the *Missio Dei*"? However, I do think that being ordained and
in secular work brings it into sharper focus, similar to how the
ministerial priesthood brings into focus the royal priesthood of
the whole church.[110]

Very likely MSEs will agree that work is (or can be) "an expression of the
Spirit at work in the world through us".[111]

There are a number of complementary witnesses to the value-based
substructure of society who serve as important guides. Hannah Arendt
in her study of work as human action points to dependability and
forgiveness as fundamental to the ordering of society as a feature of work
and human activity.[112] She explores how these two things are necessary
for human relations and society. On the one hand, we need a means to
ensure predictability in the possible chaos of human actions, especially
regarding how that contributes to the uncertainty of the future.[113] For
this there is the necessity of making and keeping promises—"*verbum
meum factum*", as it were (where the word *factum* (a work-derived
term) is as well translated as "deed" as "bond"; cf. the Hebraic "doing
the truth"). She points out that promise-making helps in relation to two
things—the unpredictability of the human heart, and the as yet unknown
consequences of an action.

On the other hand, alongside this stands forgiveness, which is about
the release from what we have done (or failed to do), and (if promises
address unpredictability) the irreversibility of an action. It brings healing
and the possibility, the actuality, of a new beginning.[114] This is deeply
about sociality, our relationship with another, for by and large promises
are made only to another, and forgiveness depends upon the response
of the other (since the one thing we cannot do is forgive ourselves). In

human action where what is done cannot literally be undone, we must seek ways of addressing the future, neither paralysed by our fear of it nor bound by what comes to pass.

Work in its creative inventiveness moves us on from the repetitive cycle of labour and consumption and so emerges a world of durability and development. But in terms of breakdown something can be mended, and new inventions and ways of working bring their own habituations in turn. Work can and does deliver progress. But nothing can work, in the sense of what society means as it depends on work and gives meaning to work, without promise-making and forgiveness. Underlying both of these, in the interstices of relationships, is if not love then respect or regard, and this is something both in making promises and in forgiving that places us in newness, what Arendt calls "natality".[115] These aspects of promise and forgiveness are not only about stability (cf. the Benedictine virtue of *stabilitas*) but about what engages the future in a way that relates to making new. These are things that not only belong and emerge within work, but they are forms of work (creativity) in themselves.

Another witness is Madeleine Bunting whose book *Willing Slaves* grew from a large email response to her enquiry as a journalist into modern business practices and the world of work.[116] She explores fundamental questions, such as why we work so hard, why we put up with it and what the cost is to our health, relationships and children. Amongst what she says we might note the following, as illustrative material for our purpose here. We might be inclined to say that, by and large, goodwill is not really a marketable commodity. However, Bunting draws attention to the significance of emotional work, which today is regarded as important as time and labour. What is prized is the capacity for particular personality traits such as cheerfulness, adaptability, being good-natured.

Moreover, these factors that bear upon human subjectivity are nurtured by influences far beyond the workplace but which are introduced into it. So, for example, "when a human resources director gives out instructions that staff are 'to be themselves and be natural' with customers, the staff's understanding of self or naturalness can be drawn from a disparate range of pop psychology, television, magazines and friends".[117] Obviously it is not only MSEs who are bringing something into the workplace from outside. Many are doing it, or having to do it.

A related key characteristic is empathy, recognized as good for customer relations. This raises the point of how and to what extent the smile is "owned" by the company or belongs to the individual. "We ask employees to bring their humanness to work",[118] essential as this now is in working styles that require emotional engagement in a way hitherto unknown when one might turn up and do the work, reserving interaction by and large for the tea break and off-job socializing. Bunting also raises the issue of how emotional labour is commodified in work, especially in so-called service industries, and how people compartmentalize human interactions as, for example, being generous to friends whilst ignoring the cleaner.[119] This leads to the erosion of human reciprocity, of what we owe to each other.[120]

She also examines how self-esteem relates to the forces of the market. She notes that self-esteem cannot be redistributed in the way income can. The problem, she says, however, is that self-esteem is not something that is a personal achievement but is the product of a set of social relationships, and many of these are in fact ordered by the state. What is missing, for example, is an awareness of just how the emotional labour of low-paid jobs in the service sector actually reinforces that low self-esteem.[121] Of course self-esteem can be damaged in other ways, not least by an exaggerated emphasis on the value of competitiveness. In a paradoxical way, poverty and consumerism can lie side by side, where constraints upon freedom of choice combined with unrealistic social comparison can be damaging. The term "loser" is doubly damaging in that it describes others as "left out", and also as having lost a sense of sympathy to relate to them. Thus emotional capital (to use an economic metaphor) is depleted. Bunting also draws attention to the language of commitment rather than loyalty.[122] This shift away from loyalty weakens the notion of reciprocity. Nevertheless, in a quote from a director in the World Bank:

> The only way to develop long lasting commitment is to tap into an individual's mental and spiritual motivations. Our mental needs are met in the realm of personal and professional growth. Our spiritual needs are met when we find meaning in our work; when what we do actually makes a difference; and when we are able to be of service. This is the realm of spiritual growth.[123]

Another witness is Alasdair MacIntyre. In his book *Dependent Rational Animals: Why Human Beings Need the Virtues* he remarks: "Market relationships can only be sustained by being embedded in certain types of local non-market relationships of uncalculated giving and receiving, if they are to contribute to overall flourishing."[124] Similar is the comment of Jeff Astley in relation to the market economy and the management of schools:

> While we need to recognize that public services (including education) are parasitic on the "business community", let us also acknowledge that those businesses are themselves parasitic on the "private services of a real community: a community that they did not create, do not pay for and have no moral right to control".[125]

The language we use of success as "having made it" also betrays a sort of commodification of people in terms of human purposing, as products that achieve a market niche. But in truth market relations are dependent on a wider social glue where there are deeper bonds at work that include the often-overlooked unpaid expressions of social care of people. There is much that is neither bought and sold, and would in fact be debased if it were traded. The social glue of humanity in its bonding holds the community baseboard together in all kinds of unseen ways.

Perhaps we can find some help on this from another direction, which has to do with the relationship between bearers and agents.[126] MSEs are more bearers than agents. This has to do with the difference between an outsider coming in, and the insider. Busking, we might say, is from the edge as the carrier or bearer of something, since the passer-by is the real agent with the freedom to respond. In ministry and at work we have responsibility. Responsibility for the MSE is suffused with the dimension of answerability to Church and God, not as an additional factor but a perspectival one, that draws us in personally since it rests on nothing but faith.[127]

This sheds light on how a) ministry transforms one's work role(s). This will shape it in ways that belong to ministry rather than work, though it is exercised within and under the conditions of work. In other words, if work carries one's ministry, one's ministry will be the bearer of one's work.

And then b) there is sensitivity to change and to provisionality, as others respond to who one is, and where one is, with whatever is being done.

And so it seems there is an important dimension of reception that is always in play. In this notion of reception the busker becomes (even fleetingly) the partner with the passer-by in some bond that has its own parameters, which are not insignificant even though they are neither dominant nor permanent; thus that which is of the moment has worth in the moment. To extend the metaphor slightly, it may be about the art of jamming. Jamming is "joining in from the edge". It is both about watchfulness to see what others are doing, and about being creative even with just a modest repertoire of harmonies, notes and chords. Ministry exists within both the episodic and the continuous, and one has to respond and be willing formationally to be changed through such interactions. Being in role may be about having control, however far one may be from "levers of power". But ministry is not actually about being in control (remember Ken Mason's metaphor of the busker at the court of the king[128]). And all this is heightened for MSE in the meeting in context of the covenantal and the contractual.

In reflecting on the baseboard glue of society, and the necessary attention it requires, a theological comment from another writer seems to be rather appropriate. "In a truly healthy society, each would see himself as partly responsible for the whole of it rather than wholly responsible for a part of it."[129] Perhaps it is a moot point whether the words "enterprise" and "entrepreneurship" belong within a distinctively Christian form of life.[130] However, there is much for MSEs to be not only concerned about, but also concerned for, in the practice of their ministry in the workplace. What matters, as MSEs themselves will know, even though it only takes us to the threshold for improvising, is asking a very naïve but nevertheless proper question: "What is the way of Christ here?" To this we now turn in exploring some possibilities for improvising with these four dimensions.

CHAPTER 4

Busking the Gospel: Improvising

In the previous chapter, we explored the dimensions or parameters that shape MSE. How these interact with each other will be context specific for each person at any particular time. But by way of an invitation to work on the shape of one's ministry, indeed to busk it, this chapter will offer six illustrations. We will consider the relationship between 1) discipleship and human flourishing; 2) ministry and discipleship; 3) ministry and human flourishing; 4) ministry and sociality; 5) discipleship and sociality; and 6) human flourishing and sociality.

The relationship between discipleship and human flourishing

Whilst the four dimensions can be related in different ways, this particular dynamic is, I think, at the very heart of MSE, and in its own way informs both the shared calling to follow Christ and the particular vocation of ordination. It brings together the two grounded realities of the framework—the affirmation of discipleship with human flourishing, posed as a question: what does it mean to say "the Lord is here"? These conversation partners require us to focus on the relationship between holiness and wholeness, between finding Christ in our humanity and our humanity in Christ, based upon the claim of Irenaeus that in the Word made flesh the glory of God is a living person whose life reflects the glory of God. But perhaps a better way of expressing wholeness in relation to holiness is wholesomeness—what is healthy. That is to say, it is not just about how the spiritual and the material can be encompassed, as it were, but embodied in the holistic reality of who we are in our daily living. It can sometimes seem as if we are looking at a hologram where we may see one way and suddenly it changes to a different picture but in a way that has complementarity.

This also extends to finding a way to interpret the often particular (and even specialist) language of belief to the language (and sometimes jargon) of the workplace.[131] MSE is about working at effective translation in these contexts, knowing that questions of spirituality and fulfilment belong centrally and equally to believing and living. And it may be even more than that in using discourse that is godly by virtue of its authenticity in its own right. Thus Deirdre Palk reflects:

> I have a professional job to do and my clients are entitled to expect the very best quality from me. That is the essential godly nature of all good work. Deacons are ambassadors for the God whom they serve, and I hope that quality of work, listening, advising, encouraging, enabling, building—as well as caring for people and making a difference in terms of care, love, justice for people—is exactly the good news that I am supposed to be proclaiming. For me, ordained diaconate operates away from the institutional church, and uses another language which does not seek to recreate cultic practices and conversations, but is a language which can be understood by the people I am engaging with.[132]

While these two dimensions have much to say to each other, this has sometimes been difficult to achieve in the history of Christian thought. For both, the contrast sometimes drawn between flesh and Spirit has made discipleship in the world and work as valued human endeavour difficult to affirm. Nevertheless both set before us the significance of our embodied existence. Today we accept more readily that discipleship is a pilgrimage in the world and not simply through it.

Of course much depends on how the Church understands itself in the dynamic between discipleship and fulfilment, and the influence this has upon the fostering of an MSE's vocation.[133] So the gospel requires all believers to be people grounded in the awareness of God in the world around us. For MSE, this may mean living with the presence of the absence of God in a world convinced of the absence of the presence of

God. But discipleship is based on what God holds out in fulfilment for everyone. It is to be shared, and it is for everyone. Questions of meaning and purpose, finding fulfilment in what we make and do are at the heart of what it is to be human. This is something to which MSE can and does make a significant contribution. Far from being at the edge of the Church as a form of ministry, MSE is actually somewhere at the centre of what the Church is about in a vision of the gospel and purposeful living.[134] Here we repeat Irenaeus' dictum that to be in Christ is to be a human being fully alive, or (as this might be expressed in a contemporary way), "Show me myself as you see me, Lord."[135]

It is no accident that the Church's envisioning of the kingdom usually expresses itself in such key universals as life, liberation, justice, love. If these are the realization of faith in Christ then equally the foundations of faith also rest on some affirmation of fulfilment, the realizing of potential for the human condition. As John Atherton wrote: "The commitment to human flourishing in all its fullness is both a human and divine imperative informed and inspired by the Christ-like God who 'came that they may have life and have it abundantly'" (John 10:10).[136] If we are made in the image of God, then faith is mapped to human flourishing. We do not turn aside from our humanity to follow Christ On the contrary, following Christ takes us deeper into the mystery and the hope of what it is to be human. This is something that we share not only with believers, as members of the Church, but with all people because of creation and the outpouring of God's love in the Incarnation. "All of us, however ordinary or flawed, have at heart a seemingly boundless longing for fulfilment."[137]

The relationship between ministry and discipleship

In their book *Being a Priest Today*, Christopher Cocksworth and Rosalind Brown root priestly vocation in relationality,[138] and affirm ministry at the interface between Church and society:

> The priest is called to support and nurture Christians wherever they may be found, helping them in whatever way is appropriate to actualize their priestly calling to be with and for others, living

in the ways of God's kingdom and practising the presence of God
in their places of work and leisure.[139]

If this is what Christians are to be and do, then priests may also surely be
found there. We might adjust slightly the opening sentence in the above
quotation to allow priestly work to support and nurture all people through
participating in work in daily life. To ask what ordained ministers at work
do more than lay people is to imply that ministry (as if it were a matter
of function) is really to do with role, and is thereby more suitably located
within the Church. But this overlooks the significance of relationality in
the vocation to ordained ministry. "All that we are in Christ and all that
we do for Christ arise from a vocation, a calling into a certain sort of
relation to him—a relationship of extraordinary grace."[140]

Moreover if clergy lead the church in worship, and that worship is
sensitive to changes in the world around since liturgy should never
be deaf to context,[141] then they can just as well be part of the world to
which the liturgy is responsive. Cocksworth and Brown also quote Michel
Quoist with reference to prayer: ". . . for everyday life is the raw material
of prayer".[142] To which we may add, ". . . everyday life is the raw material
of prayer in everyday life", whereby priestly life can engage with the latter
as much as the former. This deep root of relationality gives to ordained
ministry, as it does to the Church as a whole, the calling of a ministry
of reconciliation, which is inherently bound up with mission.[143] So the
Church that is truly shaped by reconciliation has this as the hallmark of
its identity in which boundaries are not barriers, and the energy of faith
goes back and forth between Church and world in an almost seamless
fashion. Why then should there not be ordained who in the name of
reconciliation and mission find their identity in working for a living, on
behalf of God's Church in the midst of God's world?

The authority of ordained ministry is not personal but rather
an authorization by God, who has answered a community's prayer.
Priesthood in its representative meaning is not a delegated responsibility
from the people of God—it is a gift, a particular realization (though
not the only one) of the priesthood of Christ. This gives a heightened
sense of responsibility to priesthood, in a call to a particular ministry to
enable all the baptized to renew and sustain their discipleship in Christ.

It is about a *charism* rather than function, but the *charism* is not one's own. It "lets the process flow" on the part of the Church so that God might provide. Its marks are sincerity and transparency. Sincerity is about believing that God is profoundly active in the world and is the establisher of community. Presiding at the Eucharist and serving the community of the Church and beyond belong together as two sides of the same coin in a true leadership of community (as in the foot washing in John's Gospel).

We cannot share the greatness of God by being great ourselves. Transparency is about pointing away from ourselves—so it is not a performance that subtly focuses on self. The sacrament is about living life according to the Spirit, the realization of a community walking by the Spirit in the ordinariness of washing and eating (again, it is important to read the foot washing in John in a way in which it is set within domesticity).

Drawing down the meaning of priesthood from the priesthood of Christ is a better way of holding together the MSE's ministry in church and at work, rather than trying to extrapolate out from a church context into a secular context in understanding one's ministry. This reflects the fact that ordination arises from within the calling of the whole people of God, and the way in which the clergy nurture the laity in the offering of their discipleship. The MSE extends this responsibility into and from within a work setting. In both these instances, viewed from the perspective of being an ordained minister, if faith informs one's work then it should also be the case that work informs one's faith and nurtures that aim in others. Jesus' priesthood (according to Hebrews) is that of Melchizedek i.e. a universal priesthood, which is rather larger than the corporate priesthood of the Church. So priesthood has a social dimension and is a deeply human idea—people look for others who can help them access "the beyond in the midst".[144]

This reflects the *charism* of one whose vocation is to share in the context of work, with spontaneity, acceptance of provisionality and perseverance to advance the universality of Christ's priesthood in and through the priestly life and witness of the Church in keeping the gospel alive in the world. A theology of priesthood begins with an understanding of the Church, and more properly the Church in the world, and not with clergy. The key issue for the ordained today is to evoke society's need for

God and not to maintain a group separated from society as it addresses the inter-relationship between priest, people and circumstance.

MSE is not, as we have said, a devaluing of the ministry of lay people—far from it.[145] In one form or another the Church has always had self-supporting clergy who have been employed in secular ways without any obvious inhibition of the ministry of the whole people of God. Both the revised Church of England ordination liturgy and a renewed emphasis on Christian vocation in the world have conspired subtly to focus ordained ministry within a particular ecclesiological narrative.

Again we may also ask how adequately the liturgies of the Church, particularly those of the occasional offices, reflect both a sense of our humanity within creation, and also the identity of the Church in relation to those outside who may wish to access its pastoral care. The much wider provision of liturgical variety in *Common Worship* compared with the *Alternative Service Book* is welcome, but the boundaries between Church and society have now become more clearly defined, with a tighter demarcation and a more didactic approach.[146] The parish minister may tend to become thereby the keeper of a sharper boundary between Church and society, something that may not be entirely conducive to the experience and expertise of the MSE. Nevertheless, the renewed emphasis on formational theology that draws upon the whole life context of the ordained is important. This contributes to the way in which for an MSE in a vocation to ordained ministry, the staying on at work belongs to the authenticity of the self.

MSEs are clergy who share in the life of a local congregation and, one trusts, share the experience of their self-supporting ministry with the congregation. By virtue of being rooted in a ministry in daily life, they have this in common with the congregation, namely a very large part of life experience that is distinctive and is not available to other forms of ordained ministry. Recalling the imagery of Rowan Williams, what Christian faith is about is inhabiting a "Christ-shaped landscape that is already and always part of the world; and discerning and enabling its presence to emerge within the life of the world around as we inhabit it in/with Christ."[147] An MSE's engagement with the local church will be to help the congregation to grasp this. A significant contribution to that particular task will be to reflect upon how the ministry of the whole Church is shaped through daily life and work.

In explicating the relationship between an MSE and a layperson in their share in discipleship and ministry in daily life let us explore an example that may not be altogether hypothetical. Let us assume that there are two members of the same congregation, both are nurses, one who is ordained and the other who is lay. And they work in the same hospital and occasionally meet as colleagues. (We should not assume that the MSE is the layperson's line manager!) What is the difference in their ministry at work in this context?[148] At one level, and perhaps the deepest, there is no difference. Their calling is to follow Christ and witness to their faith as seems appropriate to do so. A shared calling informs their respective roles and responsibilities.

In reflecting on the MSE as an ordained person, we have to avoid the twin mistakes of claiming too much and too little. To claim too much would be to embrace a mistaken notion of being able to do a job better, or that it lends an authority in the task. It is a mistake to proceed down that road, just as it is a mistaken view of ordination that defines it by what the laity does not do. Apart from reducing an understanding of ordination to function, this undermines the whole fundamental reality of the Church in its mutuality and collaborative ministry.

But equally it is possible to claim too little. It is not possible to restrict being ordained to the church door. If the ministry of the whole people of God exists in the world as well as in the Church the particular significance of ordained ministry in its interaction with lay Christians, and indeed everyone, also exists in the world. Simply put then, the public *persona* of the MSE has to articulate with the lay nurse in the dispersed life of the world in a way that resonates with how the ordained MSE interacts with the lay nurse in the gathered life in the church. The vocation of the ordained minister is to sign the church's faith in the gospel in blessing, reconciling and nurturing in both contexts, informed by a God-given, work-enabled mutuality and reciprocity.[149]

The relationship between ministry and human flourishing

We have already alluded to the significance of the formational dimension to ministry as this interacts with the discipleship of the whole people of God. In this, MSE should find itself both invigorated by and invigorating the relationship between vocation and living. A key perspective will likely be not simply how one's vocation exercises itself in/at work, but at a deeper and prior level, how life also shapes one's vocation. This raises paradoxically the question of what does the Church mean to me, and what is the form of the Church that is meaningful for me? MSEs have something to offer precisely because of where they are coming from, and also the fact that they are licensed to a congregation. But in the expectation of MSEs affording the Church the encouragement of ministry in daily life this cannot simply be reportage.

A Church that would nurture faith in daily life has to be both critically engaged with what that means and committed to keeping pace with it. Both of these are necessary for a world-engaged Church. What does that entail? It means on the one hand that the MSE is in a key place along with fellow Christians at work to sustain the Church in a critical dialogue with the world. And on the other hand, it is about helping the Church to avoid becoming self-absorbed and self-preoccupied. Michael Ramsey points out how the spirit of the world can invade the Church so as to subject believers to mental and spiritual overcrowding—"We who belong to the Church succumb to the world's characteristic disease of being dominated by the flux of time, and of losing the power to consider (cf. Luke 10:38–42)."[150] The MSE's collaborative concern with fellow Christians at work for godly space in daily life has much to say to the Church in its task of nurturing godly space within itself and in its life-giving faith for the world.

In this interaction between the MSE and the lay Christian both at work and in a congregation, I would like to return to what I think is a central question: how does life shape one's vocation, and how does one's vocation (to worship and serve God) inform one's life? The Church certainly has a concern for the latter. But the point is that we cannot do this, responding to exhortations to serve God in daily life, without also paying greater attention to the first part, namely how life shapes one's vocation.

The theology of baptism as a rite of entry into a new existence in Christ marks a boundary between a former life and a new one. That is surely appropriate, but as a participative celebration of daily life in Christ. If baptism is "in (into) Christ", and Christ is at one with creation (as God's Word made flesh), so our baptism "as a new creation" (to use Pauline language) puts us centrally in touch with the created order. It is odd, then, how this point is rather underplayed by the Church. The general understanding of baptism simply does not help us to value the way in which life in creation shapes our vocation to worship and serve God in Christ. It becomes almost *docetic* in the sense that, in exploring how we value the divine in our midst, the Church fills up our response, and thus displaces something of our wider humanity and situatedness. Surely the Church as the extension of the Incarnation is not for us the displacement of the central meaning of the Incarnation.

This suggests that an approach to articulating the coherence of being ordained as an MSE is a matter more of the perspectival than the functional. By perspectival I mean that the vocation of the Church in its ministry derives from the fact that the Church exists because of what God has done through Christ in the world. That is to say, God is present in the Church because God is present in the world. This is the key to understanding the meaning of Incarnation. Because the Church is also part of God's world it bears witness to who Christ is for itself as it remains centred on who Christ is in the world. In this both ordained and lay share equally, and they have mutual responsibility in this ministry. However, it is the purpose of the ordained to be the living reminder to the Church of what this ministry is, and in so far as this may also be in the workplace, then to bear witness to it as an MSE in the world.

Busking is certainly an embodied image—improvisation happens in the very nature of existence. While Paul tends to set flesh and spirit in opposition, it is salutary to note that for the prophet Ezekiel, God's gift to Israel is a heart of flesh (Ezekiel 36:26). For Ezekiel the opposite of flesh is not Spirit but stone. (Likely for Paul his contrast of flesh with Spirit is just some perception of the flesh as the self turned in on itself rather than how we are participant in the world.) For the prophet (as Rowan Williams points out[151]) a heart of stone is an unteachable heart, one turned in on itself, one that stands over against the world and community. As Williams writes, "the gift of the Incarnation is the heart of flesh".[152]

The mystery of Jesus Christ as the glory of God in human form is in the substance of the created order. This making known of the glory of God is thus through the frailty and the ambiguity of the flesh. We learn of God in the ambiguous flesh of the world, the frail flesh of the world of work in which MSE is set. Whatever else, busking is life on the street, and it is time to recover a sense of life in the flesh where God meets us in Christ, where we experience the possibilities of aspiration and finding fulfilment. An MSE presence in the world of work is about helping colleagues to affirm or discover fulfilment in work or to address the ways and means that it might become so. This is at the very heart of both human fulfilment and the Church's ministry.

The relationship between ministry and sociality

From the 1960s, when the discourse of sacred and secular was particularly in vogue, things have shifted subtly. We reflect more frequently now on the relationship between private and public. And this reconstructs what we mean by society—no longer how sacred and secular interact but how the meaning of who we are is both a personal and a societal quest in the problematic of community. One says problematic since it is now no longer self-evident that society and community are the same or even partners. Discourse about society has become possible without reference to community, and that in itself raises challenges and, it has to be said, opportunities for fresh ways of reflecting on all manner of provision to do with education, health, welfare, transport, and the habits and contexts of work. Even though this is changing in the contemporary reappreciation of community, it is still in many respects fragile.

Is it possible (in priestly calling) to look on creation in the way that Traherne or Wordsworth or Tennyson did? We might say "only just", in reflecting on how creation as the cosmos on its own terms and the created order as related to God might sustain a conversation.[153] Or we might say "perhaps", in light of new kinds of spirituality springing up all over the place as people search for meaning in various therapeutic forms. Or we might say "absolutely so", if we root our reflection in Johannine themes of glory and Incarnation.

To understand what this means a quote from Rowan Williams in speaking of the Church may be helpful:

> ... It is a place we are invited to enter, the place occupied by Christ, who is himself the climate and atmosphere of a renewed universe. Forget this, and you are stuck with a faith that depends heavily on what individuals decide and on what goes on inside your head. But if the Church is larger and more mysterious than this, if the Church is Christ's place, it is a reality shaped—not in the remote past, but daily, here and now—by Christ's action. And that action is most deeply the unbroken movement of self-forgetful love towards the one he calls Abba, Father: all Jesus is on earth is an expression of this—his forgiving, his healing, his parables, his shared meals, his death and his Resurrection. In eternity and in time, Christ makes himself a gift; and in the turbulence and violence of human history, that gift is a gift that makes peace between humanity and God.[154]

In responding to this the key themes of Jesus' message of the kingdom of God might be summarized as:

a. **Hospitality:** Jesus' ministry is one that gives hospitality—it invites in, and he rebukes the disciples for wanting to exclude.
b. **Advocacy:** Jesus' ministry reflects a concern to voice the needs of those whom conventional religion might exclude.
c. **Enablement:** Jesus' ministry expresses a dependency that sustains himself and his followers.

We cannot say what the influences were upon Jesus that led him to interpret and structure the reality of the kingdom of God in this way. We can, however, note that it was not something that arrived ready-made, as it were, independent of the course of his life. Indeed, if the gospel evidence is to be given its full weight, he came by these insights through struggle and with perseverance and in faith. If that is so, then it speaks even more eloquently of how his vision was informed by and forged through the experiences of life. This is not just a matter of knowledge but of life-shaping wisdom that has its true home in the practical realities of the world. (The above themes have some correlation with the Beatitudes: those who are poor in spirit—*hospitality*; those who mourn—*hospitality*; the meek—*advocacy*; those who hunger and thirst for righteousness—*advocacy*; the merciful—*enablement*; the pure in heart—*hospitality*; the peacemakers—*advocacy*; the persecuted—*enablement*.)

These three themes are also a particular feature of the Fourth Gospel, a Gospel that especially explores a sense of the universal working of God in Christ. The opening of this Gospel, John 1:11, speaks of hospitality "coming to one's own home", ambiguously the world/Israel, and the idea of hospitality is sustained in the verb "accepting".[155] Christ is also spoken of as advocate (14:16 "another advocate" implies Christ as the first advocate), so the work of the gospel is the advocacy of the gospel through the work of Christ. And both John 1:11 and 20:22 reflect the power of the Spirit in the ongoing work of Christ's ministry. Equally, the concept of world in John is complex. It has a range of meanings that are a) temporal (this age and the age to come), b) ontological (belief and unbelief)[156] and c) material (the Word made flesh as the context for the life of the Spirit). Here a note on world (*kosmos*) in John might be in order.[157]

Kosmos in John can represent the totality of creation, the created order (11:9; 17:5,24; 21:25; cf. Romans 8:22).[158] But in John *kosmos* more frequently refers to the world of human affairs. At 1:10, the world that is made through the Word made flesh is a world that is capable of knowing and responding. (At 12:19 and 18:20 cf. 1 John 2.2, the world means "everyone"—*tout le monde*.) It is sometimes called "this world" which may reflect the rabbinic idea of "this age" in contrast to the age that is to come (9:39; 11:9; 12:25,31; 13:1; 16:11; 18:36). But equally it is contrasted with a world already existing (8:23; 18:36). These sometimes combine in the sense of an anticipated world now in the present, and Jesus as envoy from the realm above coming into this world below. There is in John a sharp contrast between the world as it is, in the here and now, and the world that is breaking in or is above. The world hates Jesus and his disciples. But nevertheless this world is the scene of God's mission in Jesus

(1:9ff.; 3:17,19; 6:14; 8:26; 12:46; 16:28; 17:13,18; 18:20,37; 1 John 4.2), and is grounded in God's love for his world (3:16—notably here the world is split into its two components "everyone who believes" cf. 1 John 4.9–10).

There is a crisis where two seeming opposites are brought together. On the one hand Jesus is the saviour of the world and does not come to judge the world. On the other hand, Jesus does judge the world, and has overcome the world i.e. in the sense of the "ruler of this world" (12:31; 14:30; 16:11)—so those who choose to remain under his power transform salvation into judgement. Here then is the paradox, namely that the world does not recognize him (1:10; 14:17; 17:25), and yet the aim of Jesus' mission is that the world should believe (17:21,23). For John, the world does not know God and the flesh avails nothing. But it is through the Word made flesh that the world will believe. The faith of the Church in its belief in Christ is not only a concern for the world (in its material construct) but a world-contextualized faith.

The focus of the Incarnation, in Johannine terms, touches on the sacral significance of matter (itself an important point—the Word is made flesh), but is primarily addressed towards the ways in which humanity responds to God in being made in his image. Thus the stuff of creation is bound up with how we use it. That does not mean that we cannot celebrate secular sacraments, but rather that sacraments are rooted in celebration—of how we enter into the reality of God meeting us in our world.

As Rowan Williams has remarked, the meaning of the Incarnation is not just to affirm the created order as the bearer of divine Presence but also to transform it into a restored relationship with God. Nevertheless, this is about the created order as a whole. We cannot take humanity out of the landscape of creation in John's vision. The number seven has a sacred meaning for him e.g. the seven miracles; the story of Jesus in its ending (as we have seen) wraps back to the beginning where following his death he rests in the tomb, even as God rested on the seventh, Sabbath day.

The resurrection is therefore the "eighth day", the day from which Creation began, akin to the mysterious Genesis 1:5 which (in the original Hebrew) calls the separation of light from dark not "the first day" but "a day", that is to say not the first in a series but as the foundation for everything (on the other days) that follows. We are here back to the deep meaning of the tabernacle, which draws all creation in to the worship of God, and which echoes John 1:14, "dwelt among us", literally in the meaning of "dwelt" as tented or "tabernacled" (Exodus 33:7).

But going back to John 1:10 for a moment: when it says that the world did not know God, the idea of knowing is not so much an intellectual grasp but a comprehensive grasp. God's knowledge is bound up with his total mission to his world and therefore with his care and love. Thus to respond to God (1:11) is to know him in this comprehensive way that embraces his purpose for all things and through all things. Salvation is a world-related and world-focused thing, and vocation understood as God's call is comprehensive and all-involving of life.

Whilst we could translate John 1:14 (with the Good News Bible) "the Word became a human being", that does not get it quite right since it could imply, ever so subtly, a separation of us as human beings from our world. No, the "Word became flesh" means the claim of God upon the totality of the world in its God-relatedness. It is this that keeps afresh before us the eternal mystery of creation, not only as the stuff of matter but as formed in relationship to God in its origin and destiny.

Taking this as a guiding principle, it suggests that the real context for MSE in its expression of ordained ministry is a church that works centrally with the vision of Genesis 1:26–7, that human beings are made in the image of God. Consequently, this is about a concern for justice, peace, the right use of things and people, community and hope, as all this is discerned within a working life. MSE is a sign that this is what the Church is to be in its life within and for the world.

Accordingly, with this broad background in mind, we can improvise upon an MSE's ministry at work thus (recalling the key themes of Jesus' ministry):

Hospitality	Advocacy	Enablement
Blessing	Reconciling	Nurturing

This, not by accident, has a certain Trinitarian structure to it: God as Father in creation making room (hospitality) for the existence of creation in relation to God-self,[159] and the diversity of creation blessed in the relationship to its Creator; God as Son in advocacy of our true nature in

Incarnation and kingdom, rooted in reconciling all to God-self; God as Spirit at work in all the world, enabling the life of faith through word and deed, and nurturing all creation to find and celebrate in God its origin and its destiny.[160] This suggests that the Church exists because of what God has done through Christ in the world. MSE is to be in some sense a signpost for this, calling people wherever possible to "transcendence in the midst of life" and all that that means, grounded in a spirituality that need not express itself in specifically religious discourse but is yet shaped and informed by a gospel framework such as this.[161] Such a framework would help an MSE ministry in working contextually with different discourses to remain authentic and coherent.

Moreover, this framework in its Trinitarian structure is inherently collaborative. Its aim is to affirm that this is the discipleship of the whole people of God. There is no distinction here between ordained and lay. But it is the calling of the ordained to be this sign, to be the *animateur* in this calling, to attend to it in tending it as one's vocation is shared with others, whether members of the Church or not, as it flows out into the world. In this way, the representative ministry of the MSE as ordained person reflects a true understanding of priesthood, in doing "in the name of the Body what essentially the whole Body is doing".[162]

The relationship between discipleship and sociality

The relationship between discipleship and sociality, at least in Christian theological terms, involves that between solidarity and service. Solidarity takes us to some of the familiar wrestling of Paul with the meaning of flesh and body, and the Johannine paradox that though the flesh avails nothing, yet the Word has become flesh. What Paul and John reflect upon is a spirituality that binds us to the world in God's creative purpose rather than an escape from our creatureliness, as George Herbert says: "All may of Thee partake; nothing can be so mean, which with this tincture 'for Thy sake' will not grow bright and clean."[163]

John A. T. Robinson points out how Paul's claim that the body is "for the Lord" is also that the "Lord is for the body". He remarks, "He, the Lord, has identified himself with it, sunk himself in it . . . it is through man that creation failed to achieve its proper relationship with God; it is through man, the priest of nature, that the whole body of creation must ultimately be restored to that eternal destiny for which originally it was called into being."[164] For Paul, body and flesh are co-extensive. But whilst flesh denotes the world in its transient nature, body denotes its eternal significance. Discipleship in the world sets us in solidarity with everything, and it is in this solidarity that we are to follow human virtues wherever we encounter them as of God, according to Paul's exhortation in Philippians 4:8ff. Interwoven with such solidarity is the perspective that creation is made for God, and hence there is the companion theme of service.

This complex word brings together action towards others (serving) and worship (offering). In the solidarity of our existence we are to celebrate the glorious ambiguity of service (cf. Romans 12:1ff.). Service is that which addresses themes of exchange, reconciliation and transformation. We may note Paul's use of the words *metallassō* (exchange of one thing for another in an attraction to creation rather than the Creator), *katallassō* (reconciliation of the world to God), and *allassō* (transformation through Christ). Paul plays with (improvises) the idea of a movement from *meta-allassō* through *kata-allassō* to *all-assō*. The meaning of holiness and wholeness, of discipleship in solidarity and service, is nothing less than to be open to this movement.

This is not to argue that the difference between Church and society is a qualitative one. One does not have to follow a path of faith in order to be and to do good. At times, the world may be a better exemplar of goodness than communities of faith. There is always the need to recognize and affirm the glue that holds the baseboard of society together, wherever and however in the world that is discovered and discerned. Where the difference lies is in worship (as that other aspect of service[165]) in its formational significance for those who would pattern their lives on Christ, and in seeking to become Christlike. Worship is not some private activity of the religious who turn aside from the world. It sustains and directs faith's acknowledgement of the real presence of God through Christ in the world, both as its creator and its redeemer.

In summary, the holiness of the people of God is what informs the discipleship of all God's people as they live in solidarity with the world, but in a world in need of wholeness. Worship brings mindfulness that the sacramental presence of God in Incarnation is not just about affirming the world but transforming it, and such worship affords inspiration to make this a reality. The witness of the gospel, centred upon the vision of God through a fully human life, is one that requires thereby an affirmation of sociality, since individual human lives are bound up necessarily with others,[166] and God by God's own will and design (revealed in Christ) is present in the social fabric of life.[167] The images of the kingdom of God in Jesus' preaching and teaching offer symbols of a fulfilled life, one that embraces love of God and of neighbour as oneself. To uncover and discover the social reality of life in its very fabric is to encounter the presence and purpose of God. In this interweaving of discipleship, solidarity and service, worship and witness, the representative ministry of the MSE can surely make a significant contribution.

The relationship between human flourishing and sociality

We noted in the preceding section how the idea of flourishing might exist in many guises and forms. It may even be expressed informally as what "calls (to) us", indeed (even) what appeals to us.[168] Of course we cannot assume that this is identical with God. But religion may be responsive to ways in which this might be a possibility—presenting claims of faith with sufficient porosity for others to find room to make their own response. To speak of calling is not therefore old-fashioned and is probably more central than we realize. That is to say, calling actually places us at many moments of threshold, which chime in with human experience in the world. This thereby associates itself with the substructure of society in which the validation of ourselves as human beings makes for collaboration and cooperation, and the valuing of human endeavour.

Very likely the difference between an authentic and inauthentic sense of calling in the world at large is that which will draw us away from selfishness towards a social and personal flourishing, which in turn brings with it the appreciation of, and not the denial of, human diversity. An MSE ministry in this context has enormous potential, precisely because of the setting of its vocation within a wider framework of calling that exists within the world, including the context of work. This also signals the importance of ordained ministry as a public ministry, in so far as a sense of call in the wider framework of knowledge and experience evokes the possibility of people being able to share and explore, and indeed argue, with each other concerning what draws them onwards:

> Vocations then organize communities around what may be called "obscure values", signs that lie beyond the obviousness of everyday empiricism. The relationship between vocation and knowledge is reversed: a person does not decide upon an area to investigate and to give value to, but rather is summoned and compelled to learn (give worth—indeed, called into being). Knowledge emerges out of contagion and compulsion, not out of selection and disinterested choice.[169]

It is with reference to such perspectives as these that an MSE can bring the particular themes of blessing, reconciling and nurturing as the expression of ordained ministry, for the fostering of humanity in daily life and work.

We have argued that there are four interacting dimensions that frame the practice of MSE. And we have attempted to show how a personal theology of MSE may be found in how these dimensions are worked with. They represent themes that while familiar are adaptable and suitable for various contexts far from the Church, but where the Church's faith is nonetheless present. Perhaps, then, it will be acknowledged that MSE is in fact a valid, challenging and creative form of ordained ministry.

CHAPTER 5

MSE and Mission

In a number of important respects, the story of the emergence and practice of MSE contributes to how the Church understands mission,[170] not least in some implicit assumptions about the world. For example, an occasional objection to the acceptance of self-supporting ministry that people might not wish to be served in a shop on Monday by the person who had presided the previous day at the Eucharist, reflected a traditional perception of Church and society. And there has sometimes been an implicit, and at times explicit, correlation in the mind of the Church between kinds of work, status, and opportunities for influence.[171] Of course ministers come from, and therefore reflect, the membership of the Church and a relationship between ordained and professional has undoubtedly at times influenced the Church's thinking around ministry, employment and leadership. Back in 1955, as part of a revision of canon law (Canon 83 "Of the Manner of Life of Ministers"), a report outlined three main reasons for allowing clergy to hold secular occupations:

(i)   the declining numbers of clergy made a supplementary parish ministry desirable;

(ii)   that those already exercising roles of pastoral responsibility in the secular world would be that much more effective if ordained;

(iii)   that this would be a key way of bridging a gap between the life of the Church and the realities of industrial life.[172]

Historically speaking, since self-supporting ministry was introduced the majority profile of SSM oriented to a parish ministry, together with the fairly high transfer of SSMs to stipendiary ministry, has meant that (i) has to a large extent overshadowed (ii) and (iii). The laudable aim of (iii) is something of a work in progress. One suspects that MSEs have had to put so much energy into reflection on what it is to be ordained in secular employment that there has been less scope for research on working with the laity.

One also suspects a rationale that supporting the laity at work must first wait on an adequate theology of ordination for MSE, and this thereby perpetuates a certain hierarchical model of ordained ministry in the Church. The aim of (iii) also contributed to the worker priest movement and the work of Industrial Mission. Nevertheless, bringing faith and the world of work together continues to be a key and necessary part of any MSE's ministry, and the Church may reasonably expect the MSE to be accountable in this regard in the exercise of ministry.

The aim of (ii) is more problematic, in that it assumes from the start congruence between a role of pastoral responsibility in a job and ordained ministry, and it assumes thereby that ordination will somehow make this "more effective". Key to this assumption is an emphasis on ordained ministry as pastoral rather than prophetic (a point made, as we have seen, in an essay in Fuller and Vaughan's study of SSM stories[173]). It is perhaps significant that a prophetic style has been more embraced by Industrial Mission than MSE. Since the employment profiles of MSEs have been very much those of the professions, not surprisingly MSEs themselves have dwelt at length on reflections informed by the opportunities for pastoral care. They thereby establish for themselves a resonance between the work and Church contexts of their ministry, and a means perhaps of handling the gap identified in aim (iii).

Nevertheless, MSE puts itself squarely on behalf of the Church in the frontline of how mission engages with society within the particular setting of work. Some approaches to understanding MSE in this regard begin with establishing the meaning of ordination and then move to reflection on MSE. Others may leave open definitions of ordination or priesthood and work more pragmatically.[174] This raises a key point that within MSE there are different approaches to be discerned. Moreover, those who are in employment have a range of perceptions of how their work relates to their vocation as ordained ministers.[175]

Those who explore theologies of mission have expanded their threefold appreciation of presence, service and proclamation to include dialogue. This rediscovered perspective is important in light of a recovery of what is perhaps the most fundamental of values in what it is to be human, namely meaning expressed through conversation, narrative and story. Dan Hardy explores some relevant issues here in a series of essays entitled *God's Ways with the World*.[176] He notes the problem of recovering an understanding of society in a world that has known and experienced both totalitarianism and individualism. Nevertheless, "the establishment of societies testifies to a common determination involved in the meaningfulness of society as such, and this is the social transcendental".[177] This is then to be taken into the reality of God, in so far as Christian theology speaks of creation not only as what pertains to the constitution of the cosmos in its own right, but in its relationship to God and as derivative from God's own action.

By and large from the Enlightenment onwards we have inhabited a world that has increasingly worked with the former. In reflecting on the profound moral problem of the existence of society as the necessary basis of civilization, and whose existence is of central interest to the Church in the modelling of God in Trinity, Hardy warns against the danger of the Church leaping in with its answers.[178] This fails to acknowledge the extent to which a general sociality exists within the human condition anyway. The Church should not be in the position of declaring God's work to society extrinsically. In other words, the Church is part of society, its problems as well as its answers, and sociality exists outwith the confines of the Church.

One suspects that for many believers the Church is an alternative society, standing over against other forms of society and offering its vision and its gifts to them. The danger is that the Church becomes an end in itself, perpetuating itself over against other societies. The Church dependent on God in its inner life requires that the Church must also foster sociality in the life of the world, and human creativity and flourishing are integral not only to society but to sociality i.e. the bonds of humanity that make us and keep us human. It is this that keeps the Church embedded in creation. "In the old Latin form of the Mass, the liturgy concluded with the words "*Ite, Missa est*" which was mysteriously translated as "Go, the Mass is ended" . . . It really does not end, does it?

May your Mass never end. May your Mass be beautiful. Work well and for others. Your homes, your flocks, your children, your work with all things—your life. *Ite, Missa est*. Go to it. It is the Mass."[179]

The MSE is a minister of the Church in so far as the Church itself is minister of the kingdom, and it is only as the Church appreciates afresh its ministry of the kingdom (and consciously values the life of the whole people of God in the world) that it will truly affirm the contribution of its MSEs. Of course not all the world worships God, and so the witness of the Church to the gospel is essential. But the Church does this in the midst of the world "to raise up God's purposes within the world"[180] as God has made it and intends it, including its own life, which is also much in need of cleansing and healing, that all creation might praise its Creator. We may say of the Church that it is gathered in worship and dispersed in the world. This has an affinity to a prayer at the Eucharist in *The Didaché* (an early Christian document) that says, "Even as this broken bread was scattered over the hills, and was gathered together and became one, so let your church be gathered together from the ends of the earth into your kingdom" (*The Didaché* 9). The ordained minister in secular employment will preside, or as deacon will serve, at the Eucharist in the anticipated ingathering of the kingdom and go out with the people of God into the life of the world wherein the signs of the kingdom herald its dawning.

David Duke (MSE and team manager in community care) says: "My task as a deacon is to serve the members of my team and put myself at their disposal. My ministry as a manager is also priestly. To quote from Wesley Carr in his book *The Priestlike Task*, it is 'to stand on behalf of others at a point where, for whatever reason, they feel unable to stand for themselves.'"[181]

It also has to be re-affirmed that God's presence in the world is not confined to the Church, and may be found in many expressions of goodness and human kindness. And also the Church must not fall into a too-narrow understanding of the redemptive significance of Christ detached from creation. These are significant points for MSEs to ponder. Rightly understood, they suggest the difference between "Christianizing" and "Christifying"—Christianizing is to bring everything into a specifically Christian framework; Christifying is to consider all things in the light of Christ. It may be that "to make disciples of all nations" is to advance the kingdom by enlarging the Church as much as possible—but what is the Church we want to enlarge, we might well ask? Or it may be to bring all things under "his just and gentle rule", whatever form that takes, though that has to begin and end with oneself in a direct binding of spirituality and justice.

This question is as old as a saying of the Gospel in two forms—"He who is not with me is against me" (Matthew 12:30; Luke 11:23) and "He that is not against us (you) is for us (you)" (Mark 9:40; Luke 9:50). Perhaps it will not be an either/or. But even so, the dangers that Hardy points to are valid.

It is as well that MSE has been spared the unfortunate crisis that was once forced on emergent Industrial Mission in an expectation that it move from a socially engaged model to a more overt evangelistic one.[182] There is always a lurking danger for MSEs that the Church's concern for accountability might cloak some such suspicion as this, though that need not be so. Perhaps MSEs have helpfully avoided such a crisis, nevertheless, by the fact that they are (usually) licensed to a church.

Paradoxically this gives them an opportunity for witness—to the Church too, since (being part of the world) it also needs to refresh and renew its vision, and in working for the enlargement of the understanding of the Church from within.[183] However, we also need to take note of Ted Wickham's observation and distinction between MSEs who enter into work in strength (i.e. clergy moving into secular occupations) and in weakness (those who though in work may really be Auxiliary Pastoral Ministers).[184] The argument is that it then focuses the purpose of such self-supporting clergy primarily on the maintenance of the existing Church.

So, is the Church's promotion of MSE still really about "securing ancillary parochial help in the face of a shortage of clergy and money"? It should be said that Wickham's intention is about transforming the Church through mission rather than a comment about MSE *per se*. As an observation, however, it would be fair to point out that for the many MSEs who come by a vocation from within their work setting, this can lead them in creative, and at times, radical directions.

To pursue this a little further there is a potential resonance with the *Fresh Expressions of Church* movement, not least where some quite radical experiments have emerged. From the MSE literature and written evidence, it would seem that there are broadly speaking two "expressions" (to take up the *Fresh Expressions* term for a moment) of MSE.[185] Without polarizing what may be more a matter of perspective, there are those (represented by the perspectives of e.g. Michael Bourke or Robin Gill[186]) who structure their ministry as mission in terms of a going out from the Church in exploration, and a returning to tell and share the story. And there are those (represented by Michael Ranken[187] or John Rodwell[188]) who see mission as an "out there" ministry, in which new symbols and signs must be minted to convey the story of God's presence in Christ in creation and redemption. In the discussion of MSE and mission two things are of particular importance. One is weighing up the relationship between kingdom and Incarnation. And the other is about accountability.

Kingdom and Incarnation

While kingdom and Incarnation are not mutually exclusive (Matthew 11:27; Luke 10:22; John 18:36), they nevertheless represent a nuanced perspective in the New Testament Gospels between the Synoptic and Johannine traditions.[189] In the first three Gospels, Jesus speaks of the in-breaking reign of God manifest in his ministry. In John's Gospel, the Being of God is present and active in the world in the person and work of Jesus (John 1:14).

Ministry shaped by a kingdom perspective would be looking for and heralding and celebrating the Rule of God that is breaking in upon our world, changing it and transforming it in Christ. Ministry shaped by an Incarnation perspective would be dwelling in God through the Word in creation and responding to it as the very substance of our being and our creativity.

John Mantle notes the preference for an incarnational model as distinct from a kingdom model for the French worker priests and informed by the Church's understanding of ordination.[190] This is understandable in light of a wish to overcome a sacred-secular divide. After all, Incarnation signs a sacramental universe. More particularly is the importance for some worker priest traditions, especially rooted in Charles de Foucauld's mission (*présence*) spirituality, of the boyhood of Jesus, his growing up and working in the workshop at Nazareth. This belongs to themes (often developed for different reasons in the apocryphal Gospels such as the Infancy Gospel of Thomas) that give attention to whatever contributed formationally to Jesus' life in the so-called hidden years (cf. Luke 2:40–52).

Moreover, the Fourth Gospel places emphasis not just on Jesus' humanity but his frailty (cf. Hebrews 5:7–8). Thus the focus of a working life brought forth for the worker priests, in their motivation and witness, a profound significance in being with others in work that was manual, and often hard. It was an *imitatio Christi*, based upon what was, after all, the longer part of Jesus' life historically.

Perhaps we might say that within the Church it is the Incarnation model that has operated more predominantly, and the kingdom model has been one that it has applied to mission in the world. What the worker priest movement did was to take the Incarnation model and live it outward into the world. It might be that MSE is somewhere in the middle in having to work with both, in the expectations the Church has of MSE (as indeed ministers of the kingdom), and in the forms in which they express their own ministry (incarnationally) within the realities of a working life.

The shape of each of these is complementary since traits merge or combine with each other, and both contribute to public ministry in different ways. It is not that one is active and the other contemplative, nor is it the case that one is a Martha and the other a Mary paradigm (Luke 10:38–42). Indeed, Robert Barron questions this dichotomy, and helpfully suggests it is more about being centred. "Martha's problem is not that she is busy or that she is engaging in the "active" life; her problem is that she is not centred . . . What Mary has chosen is not so much the contemplative life, but the focused life."[191] While kingdom and Incarnation may give slightly different approaches to mission, MSEs can improvise with the appropriateness and creativity of both models.

Accountability

In some important respects, it seems appropriate to reflect on accountability under the heading of mission rather than (as is so often done) ministry (allowing for the fact that we can, for now, make this distinction). Accountability is about who and what ministers are and do, and it therefore depends on how ministry is understood. That being so, ministry itself requires to be set within a framework of mission rather than management—something essential, if MSE is to have a chance of being understood by the Church in the first place. In the parable of Jesus, in an illustration from the work-related world, the Unjust Steward (Luke 16:1–13) is called to give an account of his stewardship, which implies directly his responsibility. Not much talked about by commentators, but certainly there in his panic is a sense of vulnerability.

The fact that there are several different interpretative endings attached to the parable shows just how challenged the Church felt in addressing this particular story. The parable is set within a mission framework, which is the coming of God to God's own, the world. Indeed there would be no sending by the Church if there was not first that coming (of the kingdom and of Christ) that is the true origin of mission.

How this articulates with mission relates to how our modelling of God informs our faith. This rests on two things—responsibility and vulnerability. God's mission shows that God takes responsibility for Creation—God's coming in Christ is the affirmation that this has never wavered, it is part of the constancy of God, faithful in all God's words and works, the consistency of God's Truth. And the means by which God shows this responsibility is paradoxically through vulnerability within the created order. This is not the imposition but the drawing out from all that God has made of the divine response, the returning loving regard with which God loves all that God has made, including the possibility of rejection. But then we are back to the mission of God—in grace, mercy and truth God does not give up.

This also illustrates a further value associated with accountability, which is intentionality. The commitment to faith gives a sense of adopting a vowed life, that is, one within which everything is brought as an intention to serve God. In a spirituality influenced by some such value as a Benedictine *stabilitas*, accountability is an essential part of stability. It invites us to consider to whom and to what we have made commitments within the various "givens" of our life, including work. Our orientation to God is an orientation to these as a way in which God's mission takes shape within us. Put simply, one is accountable within the context where one is, i) in being glad to account for one's faith and ministry, ii) in giving an account of it, and iii) in taking others into account through it—which (see below) are all facets of accountability rooted in stability.

MSEs will be familiar with accountability in their work—after all, responsibility is part of conditions of employment. The Church can also expect some accountability for the person's ministry at work. More particularly for the Church at large—and hence the importance of MSE not simply being a ministry of the Church to the world but a ministry from the world to the Church (as Rowan Williams has already noted)—accountability belongs within the experience of the gospel:

> Most MSEs soon discover how remarkably uninterested the Church is in their work-based life and ministry. It is as if the world is just some kind of scenery against which the redemptive acts of God and our own religious behaviour were played out. But this is "the tissue of God's kingdom" (P. T. Forsyth).[192]

This comment is undoubtedly true. The subject of accountability is, however, best viewed not defensively but proactively for both Church and MSE under the heading of mission. It is an opportunity for the Church to learn further about its calling, no less, and to enlarge its understanding. Even though the Church's remit does not generally run in the workplace (unless by a chaplaincy arrangement), there is a grounded sense in which the responsibility of ordained ministers ranges out into all sorts of public settings, not only formally but informally. And it is in that informal but no less real perspective that MSE accountability might lie. In light of this, the following "mission-minded" themes may serve as a guide.[193] Since accountability is about truthfulness, which engages not only with responsibility but responsiveness, it may be helpful to bring together into a threefold pattern how accountability as truth-telling and truth sharing can operate:

1. There is accountability in a forensic sense, of accounting for something.
2. There is accountability in a narrative or story sense, of giving an account of something.
3. There is accountability in the sense of a sharing of vision, of taking others into account.

This resonates with a threefold understanding of truth-speaking as:

1. Forensic—informing by stating what is objective and factual i.e. a veracity claim = what I am telling you is evidence;
2. Narrative—informing through telling a personal story i.e. a sincerity claim = what I am telling you comes from the heart;
3. Social—informing by a process that is dialogical, and is thereby articulated within a social context i.e. a validity claim = what I am telling you correlates with a shared sense of meaning and is recognized within it.

Forensic	Narrative	Social
Accounting for	Giving an account of	Taking others into account
Truth as factual	Truth as story	Truth as dialogue
Veracity	*Sincerity*	*Validity*

It would be important for MSEs in being accountable to offer reflection that can be recognized under all of these headings, and not to favour one over another. This would help both to structure and encourage the process. And, given these virtues of veracity, sincerity and validity, it would help to focus how it is heard and received in its wider significance.

Following the above structure might give opportunity, and indeed encouragement, for weaving work and Church together. Since accountability serves as an opportunity to articulate a ministry that has much to contribute to the Church's understanding of the world, for the MSE it is about giving an account of the Church through one's ministry as well as giving an account to the Church of one's ministry. It should not be assumed, therefore, that accountability is given solely to the Church, even though the Church has ordained the person.

In working accountably, in being responsible, some values might also be in play as worthwhile and authentic. Amongst what might be looked for are these:

- encouragement
- trust and trustworthiness
- vulnerability[194]
- affirmation
- truth seeking[195]

Each of these has its own important place in a vocation to ordained ministry. They therefore have their place in understanding MSE, and should speak creatively and sensitively into any ministry in secular employment. They may also, helpfully, belong to standards in public life.[196] For the MSE, it is a matter of how these reflect the influence of the missioning presence of God, and that it is possible to improvise with these beyond an either/or of Church and society. There is a correlation between a "healthy" church and effective mission since (for MSE) belonging to a caring church can and should strengthen our life in the world. As an MSE puts it poignantly, "We share in what happens to our work colleagues."[197] It is as much about motive and inward resourcing that summons one as an MSE to make and to work at connections, rather than simply trying to balance a dual role existence of having a job and being a minister. It is about spirituality in terms of "vocation" which finds ways of integrating the diversity of life. Mission in the workplace may not mean a proselytizing form of faith, nor conveying a highly religious kind of faith but one that, as James Sweeney observes, "keeps close to the human struggle to assert the value of humanity, and a faith that seeks expression in service".[198]

In this chapter, we have considered how mission can be expressed within the workplace setting of MSE. This is itself a complex process, which depends both on the context and on how MSEs understand their ordination. Kingdom and Incarnation perspectives shape how mission is interpreted. While complementary, they have informed the vision of worker priest and MSE ministry in different ways. In reviewing accountability under the heading of mission the Church is the recipient of how MSEs discern their giftedness. Moreover, accountability understood particularly in its narrative and societal meanings gives MSEs a creative opportunity to nurture fresh perspectives on mission within the Church's understanding. Unsurprisingly this affirms the enduring significance of human flourishing for any interpretation of mission.

MSE and Spirituality

While spirituality can be a rather diffusive term, the Benedictine nun Joan Chittister describes it succinctly as "theology walking".[199] According to John Hull,

> Spirituality refers to the achievement of true humanness, and religions are the instruments for doing this in the presence of the ultimate . . . Faith is the positive response to the issues raised by spirituality or religion. In the larger sense, in which faith is a human potential for response, we may speak of faith without religion, but not of religion without faith. When faith is understood in the larger sense, faith is the attitude of acceptance directed towards the transcendence of the human, and faith in the narrow sense of religious faith would be directed towards the symbols of ultimacy.[200]

But it is also true that "we must not forget that there are forms of the spiritual which are not religious . . . When we speak in this way, we refer to the way in which art, literature, music and science contribute to the lifting of our human being above the merely biological. We must distinguish that which extends our humanity from that which transcends it."[201] This latter point is important in our modern world, in the relationship between what speaks to our deepest aspirations as human beings, and what connects us to God through the humanity of Christ as the Word made flesh. MSE is very much engaged in a conversation between these two.

In religious terms, spirituality has generally to do with forms of prayer and practice that bring us a sense of wholeness, inner calm and wellbeing.[202] In Christian terms, spirituality is related specifically to the work of the Spirit of God that animates the Church and the believer, drawing the Church and the believer into the life of the triune God and out into service to the world.[203] In other words (as with the riches of spirituality in world religions, and unlike so much modern seeking), it is not a turning in upon the self away from the world, but a search to find one's true embodied self as body, mind and spirit. It is a way to know how to love God and one's neighbour. "Mutual indwelling with God in Christ is at once the means and the end; but this is a being caught up into the paschal mystery, not absorption into the infinite, and it cannot deliver us from the sometimes unbearable tensions, dangers and sufferings of 'the world of action.'"[204]

There has in recent years been a flourishing of books and material relating to the spirituality of work, and a welcome attention in some spheres of business management to the emotional and spiritual dimension of human beings and its contribution to leadership in the work environment.[205] This is about much more than productivity. MSE and manager Michael Wedgeworth says: "The modern manager's task is much more akin to the conductor of an orchestra, working with and alongside the players, to help them create the best possible performance. But isn't this also an aspect of priesthood?"[206] On this basis, spirituality in the workplace would address that which promotes personal development, supports ethical values, encourages collaborative working and aims to make people feel valued.

This represents a valid and significant agenda by any definition. In the contribution of Benedictine spirituality in particular to the understanding and practice of work, it is essentially being called to what we do (as vocation), taking care over what we are given (as stewardship), and serving one another in love (as obedience).[207] We ought to expect that above all Christian spirituality will summon us to an appreciation of the relationship between faith and work. MSEs are especially aware of how spirituality is something that is not confined to overt religious practices.[208] Some words of Keith Rayner are apposite here:

> One of your great tasks is to discover what is an appropriate
> spirituality for people in the workplace, with all its pressures and
> its hours of work. You must not evade that responsibility; perhaps

that is the most important single thing you have to do—to come
to this spirituality first for yourselves, and then to help others to
find it through you. Such a spirituality will make the words of
the gospel come to life.[209]

However spirituality is defined, if the creativity of God is all around
us then the presence of God's Spirit is to be found everywhere. If the
Incarnation is the focus for us of God's intention in creation, so equally
our response in Christ's Incarnation is to creation as a whole; the glory
of God the Father in creation, and the glory of God in Christ the Son,
and the glory of God in us through the Spirit, are all of a piece (cf. Psalm
19:1, 33:5, 104:1ff.). And this engages us directly with work as human
endeavour. As the Jewish theologian Abraham Joshua Heschel says,
"God's being immanent depends on us. Our hearts, minds and souls
impel our spines to lift or dig, our arms to take or give, our lips to speak
good words or bad ones. God needs man; kenotically or not, he places
himself in our hands."[210] In Psalm 104, it is significant that the glory of
God's handiwork in nature and the work of man are celebrated together.
E. L. Mascall remarks, "No philosophy of human life can be adequate
if it concentrates on the relationship in which the individual stands to
other human individuals and ignores that in which he stands to the entire
universe."[211]

The significance given to imagination in this quotation is important. It
does take the imagination of the mind and heart to see God present in the
world, at times readily and at times with difficulty. But surely imagination
is part of the experience of the Spirit and thereby a part of prayer, too.
In some ways, it has to be said, the failure of the Church to support and
nurture MSE is a failure of a corporate imagination. It is also clear that
MSEs can feel under-resourced in finding for themselves an adequate
spiritual framework that can sustain them imaginatively amid a working
life. A saying of Rabbi Blue is relevant here: "Being an in-between person
I have to do justice to the realities in which I live and have my being . . .
The material world is the testing ground of all spirituality."[212] This goes to
the very heart of MSE vocation. What, then, might inform the wellsprings
of MSE in its spiritual significance? Again this will involve improvisation.

From the preceding matrix of dimensions that go to shaping a theology of MSE (the discipleship of all God's people; ministry; human flourishing; sociality), the latter two will particularly contribute to reflection on spirituality. They relate to meaning and purpose in life in the broadest terms. However it be constructed, a vocation to ordination that willingly commits a person to bring together their ministry and their place of work signals an affirmation that God is to be found in the workplace, and an attention to a corresponding spirituality for oneself, and possibly others also in nurturing faithful discipleship.

Such spirituality will embrace the many ways in which work has so much to do with human flourishing and strengthening sociality. At heart a spirituality that informs MSE has to do with the discernment of God's concern for the world and his purpose in creation. Denise Levertov speaks of "Work that Enfaiths",[213] which challenges how we should understand our creativity. God's gift to us in creation as an act of love is the freedom to choose to say "yes" or "no", so that we can say "yes" to faith and find God's love meeting us in our lives, not least in the admixture of order and complexity that attends our work.

There is a resonance here for MSEs with the Ordinal, which speaks of deacons "reaching into the forgotten corners of the world" and priests "guiding others through the confusions of this world that they might be saved for ever". Indeed Keith Rayner says, "It does seem to me that much of the ministry in secular employment is essentially diaconal."[214] This is an apt theme in the workaday world. Clergy are not above these confusions, being in the midst of them and without solutions up their sleeves, while saying "Yes" to faith. MSEs will acknowledge this readily.

It is not for the most part that work, as a particular aspect of life's experience, shapes or enhances a vocation to ordained ministry in the Church. Instead it deepens an understanding of servanthood in caring for what God cares about. Whilst this belongs to all vocation to ministry, wherever and however it is exercised in the name of Christ, for MSEs this is particularly focused on the dispersed life of the Church in the world.[215] It is no accident that MSEs retain this focus whether they are in work, or are unemployed or retired. So, perhaps, it would be better after all to speak of MSE as Ministry in Secular Environment.

In the end, it is about where one's centre is, and where one wants to set the parameters of one's vocation. "In the immense cathedral which is the universe of God each man, whether scholar or manual labourer, is called to act as the priest of his whole life—to take all that is human, and to turn it into an offering and a hymn of glory."[216] And Thomas Traherne put it thus: "This visible world is wonderfully to be delighted in, and highly to be esteemed, because it is the theatre of God's righteous Kingdom."[217] This vision, this imagination, this prayer-shaped outlook is not romanticism. It is a way of faith in structuring reality, and a giving of oneself to it.[218]

Whilst it would be impossible to try to embrace all forms and contexts of work that MSEs address, an improvisatory approach might engage with the four characteristics of busking that we discovered at the beginning. Those four characteristics are context, spontaneity, provisionality and perseverance (see Chapter 2). We can explore the metaphorical characteristics of busking that we identified at the outset (put in italics for clarity) in relation to four spiritual themes (each described as a set of pairs) as follows—place and space (= *context*); energy and focus (= *spontaneity*); desert and meeting (= *provisionality*); gifts and skills (= *perseverance*).

Such improvisation has something to do with the difference between a compass and a map. A map gives us territory in detail; even if we have never been to a place we can browse and survey the topography. But working with a compass is more immediate, something that is also internal within our selves in the way we are connected to the cosmos, a magnetism that informs the world and ourselves. The gospel is more like a compass. If it were a map, we would only have one Gospel, but we have (fortuitously, like the points of the compass) four.[219] When the Seer in the book of Revelation (like the prophet of old) is given a scroll to eat he is not munching on a map but getting his bearings. Jane Fraser (MSE and trainer and consultant in sex education) says:

> I think one of the major lessons I've learned is that there is no blueprint—no ground-map to follow. It can be a lonely and a scary path to tread, and I often wonder if, perhaps, I have taken a wrong turning. Is this the path that God intended me to take or am I being lured along a bypass by some secular concerns?

The same is true of my one-to-one encounters with people with problems. I am often unsure whether I'm being approached as a secular professional or as a clergy professional. But one thing I am sure of is that it doesn't matter.[220]

We have, in a post-modern world, to learn (like so many who long to do so) to travel light, but also to travel true. What would that mean for the Church? An answer by Karl Rahner points (compass-like) the way: "Whoever wants to live a convinced and genuine Christian life in the secularized desert where the God question is taboo must, therefore, want to be involved with God in the deepest experience of his or her person."[221]

Place and space (*context*)

A key mark of busking as we noted is location, the relationship between being at the edge and on the spot. Place and space, literally and figuratively, can take on an unspoken thought-through significance. While used at times interchangeably, we may say that space is a more abstract term than place. As John Inge puts it, "The two terms might be thought of as tending towards opposite ends of a spectrum which has the local at one end and the infinite at the other. Spaces are filled with places."[222] But equally places can accommodate spaces—those in-between gaps or intervals which are more than vacancy. A work-life spirituality informed by space will acknowledge how we structure space, represented by the span of the week in terms of days and hours, by the places where we are or need to be or would like to be.

We will also be familiar with the workplace's own spaces, physical and temporal, the many in-between locations and intervals, which in their own way directly or indirectly contribute to where we are and how we are at work. Of course working methods can attempt to mould us in and into place. Bureaucracy is in some ways a failure of trust, just as routine and rote can become damaging in the way that an habituated way of working becomes disconnected from the virtues and values involved in working with others collaboratively.[223] In modern life, the burgeoning of IT has led to a reappraisal of space—everything from microdata to intervals of time as soundbites to the growing use of virtual places and spaces. That said, Margaret Trivasse (MSE and counsellor working in the NHS) reminds us that "the Incarnation is central to Christian faith. Ours is a physical three-dimensional religion . . . Touching to reassure or comfort is important . . . lest too much of life is lived via a screen."[224] Whether we go to a place (or indeed places) of work or work from home, the activity organized around work will bring into play some particular considerations relating to place and space.

In thinking about location, one is reminded of Rowan Williams' observation that to be in the middle of something is not necessarily to be at the centre. If we imagine two connecting circles, to be in the middle of either one would never be at the centre where they meet. This in turn raises questions of where power and influence lie, since these also are not the same. Two particular moments in Scripture link centre and margin—Moses' discovery of a burning bush (Exodus 3:1ff.) and the Cross set outside the city (Hebrews 13:12). Here going to the edge brings a key transforming perspective. This is a true *ek-stasis* that can uplift and renew.

Perhaps, in centre and margin the story of the transfiguration also comes into its own—a turning aside that proves to be the heart of revelation. Jesus' going up the mountain is a story told in all three of the Synoptic Gospels (in John, Jesus is the constant revelation of God's glory). There Jesus is glorified, and equally importantly the glory of God in the face of Jesus is seen by others. The mountain, a high place, as the frequent symbol of the meeting place of God and humanity, is nevertheless a place apart, at the margin of everyday life. Of course this means discerning the focus in the midst of life's busy and bustling demands of work and preoccupations, to find the true centre. That is to glimpse what T. S. Eliot calls "the still point of the turning world",[225] to see the glory of God in the face of Jesus (2 Corinthians 4:6), and that thereby all humanity and all creation is glorious in God's sight. And it resonates with the inspiration for the worker priest movement of the hidden life of Jesus in the workplace at Nazareth where the glory of God was present in his humble origins and growing life. Here is the authenticity of the many breaking-in or disclosure moments that MSE stories speak of consistently. At this we should not be surprised, since if God and creation are bound in mutuality, if God's glory is manifest in the cosmos, then work is and can be the expression and disclosure of the divine glory. It is this that fills every context and every situation in a centred way with hope and possibility, whatever the roles and responsibilities that we have.

A spirituality based on place will require finding or making space for openness to the presence of God and others as an act of hospitality on our part, to give space to another. And going to and leaving the workplace (even within the home) within the space of the week can become important points of intention of the heart in prayer relating to a working life, and in finding or uncovering the Presence of God in seemingly unlikely or unpromising circumstances.

A Benedictine focus of *stabilitas* is actually an encouragement to this. As one contemplates something, the spaces around and between are not an absence of something but a contribution to the whole. It is not a matter of hopscotch, a child's game of avoiding the cracks, but valuing the cracks too. And thereby we can come to value the cracks within the place that is ourselves, that space where we are, both our shadow and our substance, and know God's presence in our weakness and our failures, our lack of joined-up-ness as that which also goes to make us whole.[226]

Energy and focus (*spontaneity*)

A spiritual discipline invites us to use our energies sensibly, maintaining a true sense of concentration and fostering the interaction of busyness and stillness. Pressure on time in the modern world can lead to what saps our energy and therefore to a sense of a loss of freedom. Contemplating God invites us to reflect on the meanings of God's own work and rest e.g. in Genesis 1 and John 1 and 20, where, as we have seen, Jesus' resting in the tomb is as a Sabbath, before the resurrection as the new creation of God.

This draws in the corresponding idea of energy. Jesus said that where your treasure is there will your heart be also, which implies the energy of the merchant to acquire the pearl of great price, or the urgency of the man to acquire the field in which the treasure is buried.[227] This is at the heart of spontaneity as the energy that accompanies focus. Of course in many kinds of work today energy and anxiety are twins. Apart from the common practice of short-term contracts, there is the anxiety of who is "in the room" or "in the loop", or "logging in", or whatever the phrase is, that signals concern about inclusion and exclusion, and how control is exercised, and how trust is present or absent. Putting it another way, all this is about the necessary spiritual attention given to how we can refresh our own vocation alongside others in the context of work. If our job saps all our energy then something has gone wrong. Above all else it is our responsibility to tend the vocation to find God in whatever makes life come alive, whatever sparks life into life.

Desert and meeting (*provisionality*)

Here we step into the experience of the workplace itself. This interaction between desert and meeting brings together the lived experience of working and the conditions under which work is done. In many respects, this dialogue draws upon and teases out the relationship between place and space. The varied world of virtual meetings brings its own perspective on this. The workplace may be a place of meeting that can forge a sense of community in friendship, or more one of collaboration as colleagues. Different kinds of gathering, formal and informal, bring their own deserts—lots of meetings but no community, plenty of work but little engagement, the giving of oneself to the corporate and the collaborative, but also fostering trust as a two-way street.

It is worth recalling generally just how much landscape features in the experience of God in Scripture, especially desert(ed) landscapes, or wilderness—for Israel and the prophets (cf. Jeremiah 4:23–6), for John the Baptist and Jesus, and for Paul (Galatians 1:17). And it does so for Islam, too. Desert becomes a metaphor—commuting leaves inner-city or urban contexts often "deserted" at the end of the day, the anxiety over misuse of science and technology or global warming envisages scenarios of "desertification". But taking our cue from the previous theme of place, desert is also a heart-related word that is intimately bound up with finding self, with meeting, ultimately our meeting with God. Jean Skinner (MSE and school nurse specializing in mental health) recalls:

> My work takes me into schools and the children's homes.
> However, my base is a local clinic. There is a pastoral role
> here comforting those who suffer . . . My desk is often where
> communion in the secular setting takes place over a cup of tea
> . . . I think what is interesting is that in the secular environments
> where I work they obviously see my ministry as kosher. Yet the
> church which ordained me has not yet worked out how best to
> use my skills. Many of my stipendiary colleagues are the ones that
> see my ministry and that of other MSEs as not quite kosher.[228]

Desert and meeting can be opposites—desert as a place where one meets
no one. And desert and meeting can belong together, primarily in that
deep sense of encountering oneself, reality, God.

For Thomas Merton, this interaction of desert and meeting lies at
the heart of contemplation, in "a simple respect for the concrete realities
of everyday life, for nature, for the body, for one's work, one's friends,
one's surroundings . . . ".[229] Although the idea of the desert as locus of
spiritual struggle and finding God might seem far away from civilization,
the inspiration of Charles de Foucauld led to the founding of the Little
Brothers and Sisters of Jesus to combine a contemplative life living and
working in the deserts of the poor and the deprived.[230] Significantly
the etymological root of contemplation comes from the Latin word
"*templum*", as a space for observation. Contemplation is about having
space to see, and to do this in the presence of God, which is everywhere.[231]
The capacity to see very likely leads one to an appreciation of variety and
difference.[232] This is an asset for MSEs. It signifies that this is not just
vacant space, but purposeful and engaged.

Contemplation also engages with and invites an important perspective
on time, something problematic today when busy lives leave us not only
preoccupied with time but often unable to manage it. "Passing the time"
as a phrase reflecting leisure, is almost unheard of. It is more like the
"passing of time" expressed as a worry in not grasping the moment.
But contemplation is not a waste of time, and it helps to appreciate the
perspectival importance of the present moment. To contemplate draws
especially on the faculty of imagination in human consciousness, and the
wish to find meaning not only for oneself but also with and for others.

This has especial significance for MSE—to practise, and to engage *contemplatively* with the context of work is to have regard to everything around as touched by the temple of God's presence. As Barbara Brown Taylor reminds us, "No work is too small to play a part in the work of God's creation."[233] The work-related discourse of modern life speaks of "taking time out", but this is not the meaning of contemplation, which is the formational process of seeking, growing into, habituating oneself within, God's presence in everything. This is an absolutely proper place for priestly ministry to be.

In reflecting on the provisionality of busking we may return to it here, in the experience of work. The metaphor signals, as we have seen, not a pilgrimage through the world as if the latter did not matter. Rather it is a pilgrimage by finding sustenance and encouragement in glimpses of "the glory of God in the face of Jesus Christ" (as Paul puts it) in the midst of the world, and thereby living into this destiny and this promise. The discourse of parable has affinities with pilgrimage in also being concerned " . . . not with what we believe, know or are, but what we are in the process of believing, knowing, and becoming in our lives . . . They are not primarily concerned with knowing but with doing (understood as deciding on a way of life based on a new insight)."[234]

Pilgrimage as a metaphor in this deep sense of the parabolic can contribute to the true meaning of work, one that can direct our energy and focus precisely because all human work leans upon the future. Creativity is about a venturing forward in faith and trust, that what is sown may bring forth a rich harvest. That also risks the experience of failure, and responding to it emotionally, practically and spiritually, within faith's reminder to oneself and others of the ever-present possibility of recovery, renewal and hope. Spirituality informed by this combination of desert and meeting will look to live out an active engagement in the workplace, in which truth is to be found and affirmed in honesty of encounter, and in deserts traversed through patience and the encouragement of colleagues.

Gifts and skills (*Perseverance*)

Gifts and skills will have played their part in shaping an MSE's vocation (cf. 1 Corinthians 12:7). Amongst the many significant, and indeed moving things said at an ordination service are those spoken by the bishop to deacons: "We trust that you are fully determined, by the grace of God, to give yourself wholly to his service," and to priests: "We trust that long ago you began to weigh and ponder all this, and that you are fully determined, by the grace of God, to devote yourself wholly to his service." MSEs, whether deacons or priests, as they hear these words will perhaps recall how their gifts and skills have shaped them at work, and contributed to their vocation in a vision of their ministry amongst their colleagues. Paul in 2 Thessalonians 3:5 says: "May the Lord direct your hearts to the love of God and to the steadfastness of Christ." It is to that steadfastness that ministry at work is addressed. And in Jewish thought the exhortation to "direct your hearts" is the language of religious intention to direct one's heart to heaven in all circumstance and whatever our ability.[235]

In the interaction between training, skills and learning we may also find ourselves at thresholds of creativity and new possibilities. That may mean from the experience of work in one context we move on to a new occupation, to develop our knowledge and learning within another setting.[236] In our modern world, it is likely that people will increasingly have experience in a number of occupations, which in turn invites us to consider what skills, training and learning are accumulated along the way in a working life. Of course we are invited to a right and godly thankfulness for gifts and for skills acquired, but this also deepens perseverance and steadfastness in care for others and in seeking the common good. All this then will encompass whatever be an MSE's gifts and skills for God's use and blessing.

At the heart of everything is faith. But this is as much a matter of trusting in the call i.e. the calling into one's work rather than from it. What faith believes as its tradition has to be taken into the self and absorbed and shaped by the context, knowledge, expertise and demands of the workplace. Thus faith as faithfulness commends itself as an "active patience".[237] As with busking, the MSE has chosen this path that has built into it a readiness for whatever may come as a response. That may not always be foreseen. I recall the comment of a colleague who passed me in a corridor and said, "I hear you are going to be ordained." When I said "Yes," his reply was "How depressing." This put me on my mettle.

I am pleased to remember for my own sake that my ministry at work did not conform to his stereotype and his hostility to religion, and we remained good colleagues. But resilience also has to reckon with indifference, the passing by of others who scarcely notice, just part of the wallpaper of existence, as it were. It serves to remind us of the reality of this ministry in its challenges, but also that a fundamental characteristic of improvising is resilience, something that is irrepressible.

Travelling light is also part of faithfulness in ministry. Michael Powell (MSE and university teacher in building management and a United Reformed Church minister) recalls:

> Portable ministry happens every day and all day, wherever I happen to be on the two campuses of the university . . . Pastoral care for students and staff is the strongest link between my colleagues and me as members of staff and as members of the chaplaincy team. Right from the beginning my SSM-MSE colleague and I were clear that we did not want our ministries to be separate from the chaplaincy stipendiaries. If Christ is one, then Christian ministry in our university must be seen to be one . . . It is to the URC District that I go perhaps two Sundays a month in semester time to lead services . . . I for my part believe it is these small worshipping, local faith-centred communities that are the taproots of the church; my ideas of ministry and mission would not exist if it were not for them.[238]

A related metaphor also comes to mind, one that has a storehouse of meaning for both faith and MSE, namely "tabernacling" or "tenting"—a pitching of something in that sense.[239] Thus tentmaking is not simply another term for self-supporting or non-stipendiary ministry but also a description of its character. It is not obviously the case that the Church as the pilgrim people of God travels light. The structures of the Church give an institutional context for ministry. On the other hand, it is MSE that can actually be lighter to structure, and therefore more exposed really in risk (cf. "being out on a limb"). So there is a lightness of touch in improvising. The busker, like Paul (1 Corinthians 9:18), offers her or his art free of charge, something that (as in the parable of the sower with the seed) is sown broadcast. As Jim Cummins (MSE and Welsh farmer and farm equipment "sales and service" provider) recalls:

> We do sell things—we have to or we would not survive. But the bulk of our work calls for service and yet more service with all its attendant frustrations. We are the nuts and bolts of farming, making, mending and providing for the needs of the local community. Here I listen to the customers and hope to hear God speak. I see it like this. If I am asked to preach from a pulpit I expect those who listen to hear the word of God, so why not when I speak with them face to face in the shop? And if I expect others to hear divine words through me, surely I must expect to hear as much through them. What do I hear? What can I learn?[240]

As we have seen, for MSEs their ministry is fragile, since it finds its setting in the workplace marked by rapid change, and there is always the possibility of redundancy, career moves and of course retirement. Ministry rests on the stability of God, and the commitment to the Church's faith that God's engagement with the world in Christ is a centring on reality, on what is really real, as it were. But the permanence lies there, and not in our own constructions or expressions of it. Nevertheless, if something is of the moment, then for God and reality's sake, the moment matters. Affirming the importance of the present is a way of understanding the sacramental meaning of life, the presence of God in this here and now. We cannot know the outcome of much of our ministry, but then we do not need to know. It is enough to be faithful.

In this chapter, we have explored some key themes in spirituality that inform and shape MSE, relating them particularly to the four characteristics of busking that express its improvisatory nature. They acknowledge the complexity and the creativity of such a ministry, and it is hoped that they may nurture the vocation of MSEs in affirming their ministry in worship and work. As David Jenkins says:

What does the reality of our worship then have to say about the realising of worthwhileness in all that we are involved with in our daily lives and responsibilities? How can we bring thankfulness from our weekdays to Sunday eucharist, and what power of thankful receiving expectant openness does the gift of Christ to us enable us to have on each and every day?[241]

Conclusion

This book has sought to explore and reflect upon the experience of ministry in secular employment in its distinctive quality of improvisation. We envisaged this through the metaphor of busking, noting how it resonates with key characteristics of Jesus' ministry, centred as that is on the kingdom of God. This gives the image a particular foundation for its validity. We explored how the improvisatory nature of MSE engages with four dimensions that are at the heart of the Church's identity in Christ. And in this process we discovered how mission and accountability, two topics that are occasionally addressed in connection with this ministry, could illuminate each other. And lastly we offered some reflection on spirituality attendant on the improvisatory nature of MSE.

We noted along the way that the Church might do more to support MSEs in reflecting on how their ministerial training contributes to the complexities of life in a place of work, and in helping the Church to appreciate the MSE's work-related gifts and skills. This brings us back to affirming how the representative ministry of the ordained can nurture discipleship in daily life, whilst being the touchstone of what this ministry is on behalf of the Church. The parable of the talents, the story of the one who buried their talent rather than investing it (Matthew 25:14–30; Luke 19:12–27) holds a conversation with that other parable of exhortation not to hide a light under a tub (Matthew 5:15) but to let it shine to the glory of God. MSE is about how we nourish giftedness in ourselves and in others. It is this learning from Christ that informs all that we do in the discipleship of faith and, in God's constant presence, we improvise with it in the offering and sharing of the gospel.

If anything were to be given a particular emphasis it would be to suggest that formation lies at the heart of this process—in the bringing of oneself to the venture. We signalled this by taking the characteristics of a busking style outlined at the beginning and connecting them to the features of a work-shaped spirituality in the final chapter. In the end, spirituality within a work setting is the reminder not only of work to be done in God's name, but also of God's work to be completed in the self and community. To address the former is to give oneself to the latter. This invites us to reflect on the ways in which God indeed busks his own presence within us and amongst us. The Church's mission in its discipleship and ministry is to be open to finding and bearing witness to God in everything in creation, in everyone in society, and in every circumstance of life. MSEs try to put this into practice in the experience of a working life.

Rowan Williams in the epilogue to his book *Being Human* concludes:

> Jesus has gone before us into the darkest places of human reality. He has picked up the sounds that he hears . . . He hears the human beings that nobody else hears. And he calls to us to say, "You listen too" . . . He makes his own the joy and celebration and thanksgiving of human beings going about their routine work and finding their fulfilment in ordinary, prosaic, everyday love and faithfulness. All is taken "To the throne of Godhead,/To the Father's breast" to the burning heart of truth and reality.[242]

It is there in daily life and work, along with fellow Christians in their discipleship, that MSEs find their vocation and exercise their ministry, and celebrate the Presence of God in Christ.

EXCURSUS

Jesus, Paul and Self-Supporting Ministry

In the ancient world, it was generally accepted that the divine stood behind and within the created order. This was a sacral universe, although Christianity inherited the belief of Judaism that this was not a divine world in the sense of the created order being identified with the divine. But neither for Judaism nor Christianity was the world an illusion. The human predicament, i.e. a sense that all is not right about the world, was not that spirit was trapped in the material and as a way of salvation one had to escape. Instead it was about a calling to serve God through the created order in establishing peace and justice in the human heart and in community.

In the parables of Jesus, there is a sense of the divine order within the power of nature, such as in Mark 4:28, where the seed of its own nature renders the earth fruitful.[243] Thereby Jesus is able to draw lessons that affirm both our relationship to the world and God meeting us through it. Nevertheless there is a certain ambiguity about nature, whether ordered in an intricate and mysterious beauty, or as alien and dangerous in its power.[244] Thus the spiritual and the natural remained intertwined, and the natural order would come at length to its fulfilment according to the divine will even as the work of Christ comes to its completion (Romans 8:19ff.).

Throughout Christian history there has been an ambivalence about how the natural order is to be prized as the means by which God's will is known and served. It is perhaps in our own increasingly environmentally conscious day that we are at last beginning to discover that the verdict of Genesis 1 (that God saw all that he had made as good) is the affirmation of the goodness of the world in and of itself.[245] While Christianity might eschew the idea of the divinization of nature, there are important insights into the spirituality of the material world that other world religions make, and which can serve as reminders of neglected themes in the Christian understanding of creation. It is, paradoxically, in the Fourth Gospel that we find a sense of the spiritual imbuing the physical. John's theology is antithetical to the world, but only on the basis that the world of itself cannot save itself. Nevertheless, affirmed in the Word become flesh, nature is capable of revealing the divine. And more so, grace suffuses everything so that space and time are bearers of eternity. Nature and grace are bound together sacramentally.

In the Graeco-Roman world, work was regarded as a necessity, but where it tied people down so that they were not at liberty to pursue what they wished, then it was slavish.[246] By and large, there was a philosophical and cultural outlook that the ideal was to have leisure for creative pursuits, to be in a position that one did not have to work, or to work as little as possible. In this worldview, the gods themselves did not work.

By contrast, for Judaism work was readily associated with God, both in the idea of creation and in God's doings in history. Correspondingly work encompassed both labour and observing the commandments of the Torah. As a Jewish saying puts it, "Where there is no bread, there is no Torah; where there is no Torah, there is no bread." (Mishnah Pirqe Aboth 3:18). The second, shorter, story of Creation in Genesis 2:4ff. reflects the understanding of God as a craftsman who works interactively with the material nature of the world (cf. Jeremiah 18:6).[247] Indeed almost every trade and craft serves to furnish the imagery of theism in the Old Testament e.g., the refiner's fire, the metal worker's forge, irrigation, bleaching, building, pottery, forestry and threshing.

Work can be toilsome for humankind but even so humanity praises God through work. In rabbinical commentary, the Sabbath in celebrating God as worker who rests from labours (Exodus 20:11; cf. Genesis 2:2–3) actually has the intention of focusing the necessity of work. Nevertheless, there gradually emerges a certain preference for that especial work which is the study of Torah. And in time, there is an appreciation of being able to study without the distractions of labour. It is in the wisdom tradition particularly (Wisdom 38:24–39:11) that we find a contrast between different occupations and that of the scribe.[248]

Some of this no doubt contributes to a criticism of Paul in choosing to work for a living. The preference within the wisdom tradition for not having to work echoes in some respects a similar outlook in the Graeco-Roman world. However, for the scribes and rabbis it was not a matter of having more free time at one's disposal for other pursuits, but of time to devote to the study of Torah, and hence delight in meditating on God's Law day and night.[249]

Jesus grew up and learned a trade of carpentry (Mark 6:3; cf. Matthew 13:55) that likely included building as well (in the meaning of *"tektōn"*), which gives Mark 13:1–2 a particular poignancy. But he left his work and he called his disciples away from their occupations (with what consequences for family income and other responsibilities we cannot discern). This was not a privileging of the spiritual over the material, but the urgency of response to what he understood as the in-breaking of the kingdom of God. And since all obligations, work included, stood under the claim of faith to serve God, the mission of the kingdom could be understood, paradoxically, as the heightening of that obligation.

On the other hand, later on, as the Church emerged and had to come to terms with its historical and organizational significance in maintaining the mission of Jesus, it is clear that a certain adaptation emerged. The general recovery of the obligation to work as the expression of faith and responsibility is set alongside a realization that for some there was a higher work (rather akin to the Jewish wisdom tradition), of devoting oneself to the mission of the Church and the work of care for emerging congregations, and being supported by them. In practical terms, the emergence of a supported ministry, signalled in Galatians 6:6, became a necessity.

In its time, the mission strategy of Jesus was one suited to a rapid and widespread proclamation of his belief in the coming kingdom of God. It was thoroughly pragmatic in that it presupposed a light but organized means of advancing his ministry. The practice of relying on the care of others is not unrelated to Jesus' own custom of accepting and enjoying hospitality (so especially Luke 8:3; Matthew 27:55; cf. Matthew 11:19 and Luke 7:34–6), and to the fact that the disciples as a group had a communal purse or money box (John 12:6 and 13:29), a custom not uncommon at the time, for the purposes of providing charity and receiving support.

A further clue is to be found in the Passion Narrative in the ease with which a room for the Last Supper was arranged, obviously drawing on a network of contacts forged through a spreading reputation. Receiving support also affirmed a reliance on the providence of God through trusting in the provision of others (Matthew 10:5–14). In due time, it gave rise to a proverb, either taken up by Jesus or reminted by him, that "the labourer is worthy of his hire" (cf. Matthew 10:10; Luke 10:7; 1 Corinthians 9:14; 1 Timothy 5:18; cf. Didaché 13:1–2).[250]

However, not every would-be follower of Jesus was required to give up their daily life and undertake a peripatetic ministry—occasionally people were enjoined to proclaim the gospel within their own circumstances. It was also natural for some of the disciples to return to their daily occupations in the aftermath of Jesus' death. In other words, the messianic movement had not at that stage permanently disconnected the disciples from a former way of life. In the recommissioning of the disciples in light of the resurrection the peripatetic reliance on others is renewed, echoed perhaps in the communalism of the early Church in Jerusalem as recounted in Acts 2:44–7.[251] This strategy would work in founding churches in Jewish communities and synagogues, where a missionary enterprise could be extended through absorption within Jewish faith and life. (We should not necessarily assume that all churches were separate communities. They might be messianic groups within the parameters of Judaism.)

But a different strategy would be called for in light of a mission to the Gentiles. Whilst funds might have been available for advancing the Church in new settings, a self-supporting style of ministry would be important, if not necessary, prior to the establishing of a faith community. (It would also have come about in response to a need for teaching and interpretation in the churches centred on a growing body of faith-related material.) This strategy in founding the Gentile Church indicates Paul's (and others') pragmatism in pursuing an apostolic mission. Paradoxically, it is precisely such self-support that resonates with the practicality of Jesus in his strategy of relying on others. In other words, far from contrasting Jesus and Paul on this point we should reflect on a deeper underlying unifying pragmatism.

That Paul's self-supporting apostleship was a matter of deeply held conviction is clear not only from the exemplary significance he makes of it (2 Thessalonians 3:7ff.), and the vigour with which he defends it

(2 Corinthians 11:7–15 and 12:13–16; cf. 1 Corinthians 9:1ff.), but also from the simple fact that he chose this way for himself. Why he did so, and thus did not make use of a right to church support, which he acknowledges he could claim (1 Corinthians 9:4ff.; 2 Thessalonians 3:9), may have been due to a number of factors, and not just one in particular. It would, for example, have enabled him (and Barnabas) to pursue a particularly effective pattern of mission within the cosmopolitan nature of the Ancient World.[252] Again, Paul's Jewish background places him in the tradition of scribes who, by practising a craft as a means of economic independence, could take pupils without charging them.[253]

It was also the case that amongst moral philosophers, providing teaching free of charge was the mark of a truly wise man, e.g., "I generally do not regard it right to make money from philosophy, and that goes for me, especially, since I have taken up philosophy on account of the command of God" (Pseudo-Socrates Epistle 1:1–2). Some philosopher teachers, particularly in the Cynic tradition, also undertook work. This accorded with a deliberately provocative style of presentation and forthrightness in a class-conscious world, in which (as we have seen) work tended to be aligned with slave status. Even so, amongst the philosophical schools, work was generally the least popular option as a means of livelihood compared with charging fees, entering the household of a wealthy patron or simply begging.[254] For many philosophers, manual labour was demeaning, echoed perhaps in a sentiment expressed by Paul himself at 1 Corinthians 9:19, "I have made myself a slave to all," and at 2 Corinthians 11:7, "abasing myself . . . because I preached God's gospel without cost to you".[255] Paul also links his self-supporting ministry to a sense of independence (1 Corinthians 9:1ff. and 9:19ff.) in that he chose to interpret the grounds for, and the privileges attaching to, apostolic office in his own way.[256] Nevertheless this independence which he claimed, a value also prized by moral philosophers of his day, was not to avoid his teaching being compromised through indebtedness, but in order that he might be free to fulfil an apostolic care for his churches by not being a burden upon them.

Paul (like Prisca and Aquila[257]) was a leather worker (Acts 18:2–3), taught by his father in fulfilment of expectation that a son should learn a trade. He came from Tarsus in the Roman province of Cilicia. The

city was a centre of the leather and felt industry—so much so that the
Latin *"cilicium"* referred to the felted goatskin which was used to make
tents and cloth. We might assume (as with the trade of Simon the tanner
in Acts 1:6) that such a trade was viewed as ceremonially unclean, but
Berakoth 63a says that tent making was "a clean and not laborious
trade". (That latter comment about "not laborious" may not entirely fit
with Paul's statement about the hardships of his trade, if the hardship
is interpreted with reference to the manual work itself, as distinct from
a reference to either long hours or facing the criticism of others about
being "virtually a slave".)

Paul moved from Tarsus to Jerusalem to undertake formal study with
Gamaliel I and no doubt did so because of being recognized as a pupil
of great potential and who would benefit from one of the greatest of
teachers of the day. Perhaps he did this at the age of twelve to thirteen
(at *bar mitzvah*, depending on how we read Acts 22:3). It may well be
that at this point he was influenced by the current view of full-time study
of Torah as an option preferable to combining this with a trade. If that
was so, he then reverted to being self-supporting when he had to find a
means as a Christian missionary to survive in the Graeco-Roman cities
of the Empire.

It was the very expansion of the Church that brought communities
into being which could and did render support to apostolic mission, both
for itinerant missioners who visited churches (cf. Matthew 10:40–2), and
for such as Paul who occasionally received support from others (notably
the church at Philippi). In reflecting on the connection between the
proverb alluded to by Jesus ("the labourer is worthy of his hire") and the
emerging church's adoption of ministerial support, it is worth pausing to
ask how in fact the connection came to be sustained. That is to say, Jesus'
mission in sending out the Twelve (and, for Luke, the Seventy) was in
the context of eschatological urgency. On the other hand, the Church's
practice of a supported ministry grew from a different need i.e. its own
emerging historical existence. Here an adaptive response to circumstance
is in evidence. Although the Church remembered the injunction of Jesus,
we may ask what other factors were involved in the reapplication of this
saying to the Church's own developing existence. There is a transition
to be noted in the process of transmission, whereby Jesus' command in

its ahistorical eschatological urgency is now addressed to the life of the Church in its continuing historical continuity. This question is also worth asking because (in the wider Gentile world at least) there was no general custom of financial support for religious teachers. Thus it is noteworthy (if we may put it this way) not that a self-supporting ministry developed but that a church-supported ministry actually continued and grew.

In light of the foregoing, we may summarize the following reasons within the Church for the retention of Jesus' saying, now applied to its own faith setting. Reference is made, in part, to what can be gleaned indirectly from what Paul says about "the right of an apostle" to church support.

a. An appeal to what is "reasonable"—at 1 Corinthians 9:7 the "reasonableness" of a supported ministry is implied through a succession of images: the soldier who expects to be maintained for his service, the vinedresser who expects to be nourished from that on which he bestows his labour, and the shepherd who reaps a reward from the flock that is cared for. We may note that all of the images in verse 7 are drawn from the world of work, echoing the reference to the mention of Paul's and Barnabas' own work in verse 6, but now applied to the reasonableness of the Church to support the "work" of its own ministers on its behalf. Paul ironically follows the logic of his own argument by showing that he does himself gain a reward for his work, which is the Corinthians themselves (9:11–12).

b. The influence of a kind of received general wisdom as aphorism. "Let him who is taught the word share all good things with him who teaches" (Galatians 6:6). ("All good things" implies a sharing of material goods as well as in spiritual matters.) We have noted that this is likely the earliest reference to the emergence of a supported ministry. Paul makes the point that no one should be excluded from exercising a gift in ministry by not earning enough to support themselves. It also suggests that since teaching is the core of the work (cf. the extent to which the early Church was built around "the Word"), a significant body of learning, and the time needed for instruction in it, was emerging in the Church as a time-consuming activity. Thus a supported ministry began, in effect, for practical reasons.[258]

c. An appeal to experience—to common sense is added common practice. This is again expressed at 1 Corinthians 9:7 in the repeated "Who?" which in the original is an emphatic "Whoever?" i.e. this is the commonly accepted practice and experience of daily life.

d. The reference to wider custom—to return to 1 Corinthians 9:13 the opening phrase, "Do you not know . . . ?" implies a possible broad acquaintance with liturgical practice not only in Judaism but also in Paganism. Significantly (as with the images from the world of work at 9:7) it is exactly the same word (*"ergazesthai"*) for "officiate" here that Paul also uses of his secular work/employment at 9:6. Thus it is equally "work", whether it is ministerial care within the church that is being talked about, or a job in daily life.

e. The influence (possibly) of the communal nature of the early Church in the sharing of resources and support—"All who believed were together and had all things in common" (Acts 2:44).

f. The use of Scripture—e.g. in the quotation from Deuteronomy 25:4 ("You shall not muzzle an ox while it is treading out the grain") at 1 Corinthians 9:9 and 1 Timothy 5:18. Thus Scripture may be used to complement the saying of Jesus.

It is notable how many of these claims arise from general principles relevant to daily life, whether as an appeal to reason, or to custom, or usage. This reinforces the importance of pragmatic and improvisatory considerations. Such principles as these enabled the Church to transpose the eschatological context of Jesus' missionary command in the coming of the kingdom into its own historical mission in the life of the surrounding world.

We may surmise that if it was a matter of an adaptive process that enabled the Church to recollect conveniently a saying of Jesus for its own existence, there was enough leeway for Paul and others to follow an alternative strategy of mission, by which they had themselves helped to bring the Church into existence. And by holding to it as a practice they found essential meanings in what it was to live by the gospel and to nurture the Church.[259] Exploring the understanding of work in Paul encounters a range of meanings, e.g. human endeavour in general (often viewed as subject to weakness); observances of the law—its doings; the work of the gospel in apostolic ministry; Paul's own self-supporting ministry; endeavour within the Church as the expression of discipleship. It is difficult, perhaps, from such a diverse range of scattered references to construct an overall theology of work in Paul. Nevertheless, as a working apostle (in a self-supporting sense) Paul affirmed this practice as an important means of furthering the apostolic mission of the gospel, and as it contributed to the maintenance and stability of the churches he founded.

Paul's letter to the Philippians, and especially chapter 4, provides an interesting and delicate perspective on how the issue of funding relates to Paul's strategy. The following, as a case study, is a summary of the main points. The letter to the Philippians was written from prison—perhaps Ephesus rather than Rome. If this was the case, then the issue of money was much on Paul's mind as evident from the Corinthian correspondence, including the collection in 1 Corinthians 16:1ff. Paul had to be absolutely scrupulous in ensuring that this was not for himself. The Philippians had sent Paul a gift of money. We need to remember that someone put in jail in those days was not fed or looked after, and jail was a place where one was put whilst the authorities decided what to do. To survive one needed friends (Matthew 25.36). Epaphroditus had been sent with the gift (2:25). It was about a week's journey from Philippi to Ephesus, and moreover he had fallen ill. Paul is obviously concerned both about him, and also to assure the Philippians that the money had indeed reached him, and that it had not gone missing.

Paul is also anxious to be seen as independent, but at the same time to show that he is deeply grateful for the Philippians' support. 4.10–14 frames the point: verse 10 and verse 14 = it was really good to receive what has been sent. But the middle section here is a courteous reminder nevertheless that he did not really absolutely need this gift (for all the strictures of being in jail). In other words, Paul's fellowship with them is something for which he is profoundly grateful, but it does not mean he is absolutely dependent on them, lest anyone think he is in anyone's pocket, so to speak (as another but different sort of financial metaphor!). So verse 10b is guarded but also generous in its warmth.

Verse 10: "you have revived" conveys the idea of "springing to life" as a root image of renewal and vigorous hope. There are parallels to our passage with what he has said earlier in the letter 2:19–30 (cf. similar themes of rejoicing, having concern, being in want, sharing and the gospel as God's glory).

Paul's expression of joy is the key context within which he reflects on all he has to say about financial support given to him. Moreover, joy is not just about emotion but primarily about what one does i.e. making sure that action flows from the heart. It is not (just) about being happy but about celebration—it requires that around which one has to do some organizing and making it evident. As a background to the letter, people at large celebrated Caesar's lordship publicly, and Paul here conveys the idea of a counter-witness, which also has to do with public truth. One might draw a parallel with Acts 16:25 and singing hymns and proclaiming the word to fellow prisoners and jailors at midnight in a cell.

Verses 11–13: "content"—here Paul probably takes up a secular (Stoic) philosophical idea of being self-sufficient. By comparison, Paul transposes it into a Christian frame of reference by which he means, "I can do all things through him who strengthens me"; cf. verse 13 in its meaning of being totally reliant on Christ. Philippians 4:11–13 clearly indicates that (like the disciples in the mission on which Jesus sent them) he was totally reliant on God's mercy.[260]

Verse 12: "I have learned the secret" perhaps reflects the background of the mystery cults = "I have been initiated into". Paul is saying, "I will tell you the secret," which is the insight both of going without and coping with abundance as a spiritual discipline, itself rooted in joy (cf. verse 10 earlier). Of note is the fact that Paul is exploring faith by drawing upon some quasi-technical terms that were around in public (moral/religious) discourse.

For Paul, it is a matter of acknowledging his independence but all within the context of Christ. And what all this looks like (he says) is a *koinōnia* = a real sharing and partnership in Christ.

Verse 14: "share" is in its core meaning of fellowship a matter not so much of a warm impression but more a business partnership (again an appropriate metaphorical derivation in financial terms). At root, fellowship is in tune with love, where abundance helps the needy. Recollecting Acts 2:44–5, the practice of sharing in the Jerusalem church was not a glorious failure. It was not motivated by a social experiment in selling up all they possessed but expressed the obligation of help. In other words, it was about fellowship as an absolute duty to living as a shared family in looking after each other, and possibly others too (Luke 6:30–6).

Verses 15ff.: Paul comes back to the special connection he has with the Philippians and the region of Thessalonica. He has a special affection for these churches. Indeed, he holds up the northern Greek churches in their poverty to the wealthier Corinthians—his support has come from the poorest of his congregations.

Verse 17 returns to an underlying theme i.e. "just to be clear—I was not asking for this support for myself as if I were getting rich by means of the gospel".

Verse 18: "I have been paid in full"—anything owing to me in this fellowship is more than fully paid off. Our mutuality is assured and deep.

Paul then switches the imagery to cultic metaphor. We are too used to sacrificial imagery as applied to effort (e.g. "a bit of a sacrifice to do this"). But what Paul really means is that the good things in the gospel, material and spiritual, are being "offered" i.e. given away.

Verse 19 shows Paul's effortless change of gear from the spiritual to the financial.

Verse 20: Paul offers this doxology as a heartfelt affirmation of God's glory shown in everything, practical and spiritual.

By way of summary, the overall theme of the letter is about letting one's public life express the gospel so that anyone can see the nature of Christian faith. The core is in the self-giving of Christ in 2:5ff. This is then paralleled for Paul himself in giving up everything (3:7–8), and is further paralleled in the fellowship of the Philippians with Paul, in a similar commitment to sharing and participation that is at work in them both. It is this that frames the delicate way in which Paul broaches the matter of funding for ministry in a mixture of expressing gratitude without seeking to take advantage, and of mutuality that affirms reliance upon Christ. Throughout, there is the constant belief in God's glory being revealed.

Turning now to the Corinthian correspondence, we can suggest the following reasons for Paul's practice:

- because he could not have relied on church support since (at least to begin with) it was the task of mission to establish a congregation first of all (cf. Acts 18:1–3).
- because he did not want to be a burden on a congregation (1 Corinthians 9:4; 2 Corinthians 11:9; 1 Thessalonians 2:9; 2 Thessalonians 3:8). This point articulates with the previous one in that if Paul's congregations drew upon the urban poor, it would have been a source of suspicion if it was thought that Paul's intent was to found a body that would be expected to support him.[261]
- because it set a good example (Acts 20:34; 1 Thessalonians 2:11; 4:11; 5:4; 2 Thessalonians 3:9).
- because it gave him a sense of independence (1 Thessalonians 5:12).
- because it enabled him to follow the principle of offering the gospel "free of charge" (1 Corinthians 9:18).
- because it enabled him to embody the significance of God's self-giving love in Christ (2 Corinthians 8:9—noting the "economic" hint in the text). Whether this could be extended to Paul's sense of identification with an artisan class per se is uncertain.[262]

It is significant and salutary that there was no one single reason why Paul exercised a self-supporting ministry. This is an important point when (as we have seen) the theology that informs and sustains MSE often remains interiorly complex and diverse. Of note, however, from two further texts (2 Thessalonians 3:7–13 and Ephesians 4:28[263]) is the suggestion that for Paul his work as a self-supporting apostle is very much related to the wider wellbeing of the Church. Absent from this list, unless it be found within the exemplariness of work (cf. 1 Thessalonians 4:11 "work with your hands, as we directed you"), is the idea of the creativity of work. Paul's view of work is essentially that it is hard, even though it does allow him insight into the meaning of God's purpose in Christ. Even the possibility of the workplace as a focus of missionary activity (1 Thessalonians 2:9) does not lend itself to explicit appreciative comment about mirroring the divine image of the creator as craftsman and in celebrating work as creative, such as is found in some rabbinic texts, and in some theologies of MSE.[264] But given that the context of Paul's letters is exhortation to congregations, the absence of references to honouring God through practising a trade does not mean that Paul did not share that particularly Jewish view of the relationship between human action and divine service.

Summary

In deciding to be self-supporting Paul, as we have seen above, was opting for a pattern that many other teachers would not have followed. Since work had slave-status in cultural norms, many philosophers and teachers preferred to find employment in a household or even to beg. On the other hand, as we have also seen, a supported ministry began to emerge early in the Church, likely under the impetus of a need for those who could provide teaching and guidance in a focused way, and which found support in a tradition that could claim the authority of Jesus. Thus Paul himself quotes at 1 Corinthians 9:14 a "word of the Lord" whereby "the labourer is worthy of his hire" (cf. Matthew 10:10 and Luke 10:7–8 with Galatians 6:6). To be sure Paul also did himself receive support from the Church (so Philippians 4:14ff.; cf. 2 Corinthians 11:8), but his practice of not being a burden held good in that he did not seek support from a congregation where he was based at the time.

Nevertheless in following a pattern of self-support Paul incurred serious criticism. It is clear that certain members of the congregation adversely compared Paul's self-supporting ministry with those apostles who were supported by the Church. Very likely for them, Paul's chosen practice showed both that he did not trust himself sufficiently to the providence of God (as Jesus himself had advocated), and also that he was not sufficiently committed to the Church in its hospitality. It also likely reflects some popular Graeco-Roman attitudes to work as slavish. This shows the potential theological and pragmatic pitfalls Paul had to wrestle with as a consequence of his own apostolic strategy. After all, had not Jesus said as much in Matthew 6:28b about the lilies of the field which "neither toil nor spin" (and the word "toil" is exactly the same word Paul uses at 1 Corinthians 4:12 about the hard graft of his own work); and had not Jesus also invited the young man at Mark 10:21 to "go, sell what you own . . . and you will have treasure in heaven"? Thus (cf. Acts 2:44–5) there was a ready perspective and incentive in the Church towards apostles seeking the support of the Church. Whilst Paul, as we have seen, was not the only self-supporting evangelist, none the less the practice of remaining self-sufficient was likely against the trend in the Church basing itself on the disciples' pattern of "leaving all behind" and following Jesus.

However, Paul's practice of self-support gave him every authority to speak to the church at Thessalonica where (possibly) in expectation of the *parousia* some had given up work altogether. Paul takes them to task for reneging on their responsibilities to earn their own keep. After all, it might be one thing for apostles to expect not to have to work and enjoy the support of the church. But it was another thing for members of the church to behave like that. To extend the practice of apostolic support in this way meant structural collapse!

Also more widely, and not to be lost sight of, there were other forms of ministry in a congregation. And there is no indication that these people did not earn a living in the usual way.[265] Indeed Paul's use of the term "fellow worker(s)" whether as noun or verb suggests a seamless inclusion of peripatetic and local leaders who would have supported themselves.[266] Across the history of the Church there were many who helped to nurture, shape and guide congregations who would undoubtedly have continued to support themselves.

Overall, then, it can be seen that the Church in its discipleship and ministry was evolving pragmatically. The Church looked back to the tradition of Jesus while also responding in different ways to ideas and practices that were part of the world into which it was emerging. This brief but expansive time in Christian origins was marked by improvisation in the development of its ministry.

Bibliography

Allen, R., "The Case for Voluntary Clergy: an Anglican Problem", *The Interpreter* (July 1922), pp. 314ff.

Arendt, H., *The Human Condition* (Chicago: University of Chicago Press, 1998).

Aspinall, P., "Condemned to Insecurity?" *Ministers-at-Work: The Journal for Christians in Secular Ministry* 143 (October 2017), p. 27.

Astley, J., "Christian Values and the Management of Schools", in W. Kay, W. and L. J. Francis (eds), *Religion in Education* (Leominster: Gracewing, 1998), pp. 353–86.

Atherton, J., *Marginalization* (London: SCM Press, 2003).

Austin, M., "Towards a Secular Ministry", J. Fuller and P. Vaughan (eds), *Working for the Kingdom: The Story of Ministers in Secular Employment* (London: SPCK, 1986), pp. 108–16.

Baelz, P., "Ministers of the Kingdom", in P. Baelz & W. Jacob (eds), *Ministers of the Kingdom* (London: CIO Publishing, 1985) pp. 32–40.

Barenboim, D., The Reith Lectures (2006).

Barker, J., Radio Leeds, "One on One", 8 January 2013.

Barker, M., *The Hidden Tradition of the Kingdom of God* (London: SPCK, 2007).

Barrett, C. K., *The Gospel According to St. John* (London: SPCK, 1965).

Barron, R., *The Strangest Way: Walking the Christian Path* (Maryknoll: Orbis, 2015).

Barton, S. C., "New Testament Interpretation as Performance", *Scottish Journal of Theology* 52:2 (1990), pp. 179–208.

BBC News Business, "The Rise of 'Presenteeism' in the Workplace" (14 April 2019).

Beckett, Sister W., *The Art of Lent: A Painting a Day from Ash Wednesday to Easter* (London: SPCK, 2017).

Bennett, R., "The People of God", in P. Baelz & W. Jacob (eds), *Ministers of the Kingdom* (London: CIO Publishing, 1985), pp. 41–6.

Blue, L., *Best of Blue* (London: Continuum, 2006).

Borg, E., "An Expedition Abroad: Metaphor, Thought and Reporting", *Midwest Studies in Philosophy* 25:1 (2001), pp. 227–48.

Bourke, M., "The Theology of Non-Stipendiary Ministry", *Theology* 84 (1981), pp. 177–82.

Bromiley, G. W., *Theological Dictionary of the New Testament Volume III* (Grand Rapids, MI: Eerdmans, 1965).

Brown, C., "A Brief History of the Development of Non-Stipendiary Ministry and some Commentary on the Current Situation", in *On the Boundary: Reflections on Non-Stipendiary Ministry* (Diocese of Chelmsford, 2002), pp. 4–7.

Buber, M., *Tales of the Hasidim: The Early Masters* (New York: Schocken Books, 1975), pp. 262–3.

Bunting, M., *Willing Slaves: How the Overwork Culture is Ruling our Lives* (London: HarperCollins, 2004).

Church of England, *Stranger in the Wings: A Report on Local Non-Stipendiary Ministry* (London: Church House Publishing, 1999).

Church of England, *For Such a Time as This: A Renewed Diaconate in the Church of England* (London: CIO, 2001).

Church of England, *The Mission and Ministry of the Whole Church: Biblical, Theological and Contemporary Perspectives*. GS Misc. 854 (London: Church House Publishing, 2007).

Clark, C. G., "A Rumour of Priests", *Theology* 92 (1989), pp. 20–5.

Cocksworth, C. and Brown, R., *Being a Priest Today*, second edition (Norwich: Canterbury Press, 2006).

Conradi, P. (ed.), *Iris Murdoch: Existentialists and Mystics* (London: Penguin, 1997).

Cummins, J., "The Holiness of the Mundane", *Personal Communication*, 8 August 1999, pp. 1–14.

Cundy, I., "Word and Sacrament: Ministry of the Word", in P. Baelz & W. Jacob (eds), *Ministers of the Kingdom* (London: CIO Publishing, 1985), pp. 52–61.

Davies, D., "Person, Power and Priesthoods", in J. Fuller and P. Vaughan (eds), *Working for the Kingdom: The Story of Ministers in Secular Employment* (London: SPCK, 1986), pp. 93–101.

Davies, D., *Private Passions: Betraying Discipleship on the Journey to Jerusalem* (Norwich: Canterbury Press, 2000).

Davis, J., "Lay and Ordained in the Workplace", in J. Fuller and P. Vaughan (eds), *Working for the Kingdom: The Story of Ministers in Secular Employment* (London: SPCK, 1986), pp. 74–9.

Deane-Drummond, C., *A Primer in Ecotheology: Theology for a Fragile Earth* (Eugene, OR: Wipf and Stock, 2017).

Diocese of Southwark, *Towards a Theology of Ministry in Secular Employment* (1997).

Donovan, V. J., *Christianity Rediscovered* (London: SCM Press, 2001).

Duffy, E., *Walking to Emmaus* (London: Burns & Oates, 2006).

Duke, D., "Standing on Behalf of Others", in J. M. M. Francis (ed.), *An Ordinary Way of Life: Portraits of Self-Supporting Ministry in the Diocese of Durham* (1999), pp. 29–30.

Dundas, G., "Sausages and sermons on offer as butcher becomes priest", BBC News Derby, 5 November 2011.

Dunn, J. D. G., *The Epistle to the Galatians* (London: A. & C. Black, 1993).

Eaton, J., *The Contemplative Face of Old Testament Wisdom (in the Context of World Religions)* (London: SCM Press, 1989).

Eliot, T. S., *Four Quartets* (London: Faber, 1959).

Erlander, L., *Faith in the World of Work: On the Theology of Work as Lived by the French Worker-Priests and British Industrial Mission* (Uppsala: Uppsala University, 1991).

Fagles, R., *Homer, The Odyssey* (New York: Penguin Books, 1996).

Falx, Marcus Sidonius with Jerry Toner, *How to Manage Your Slaves* (London: Profile Books, 2015).

Forshaw, E., "Industrial Chaplaincy and Ministry in Secular Employment", in J. Fuller and P. Vaughan (eds), *Working for the Kingdom: The Story of Ministers in Secular Employment* (London: SPCK, 1986), pp. 67–74.

Fox, M., *The Reinvention of Work: A New Vision of Livelihood for Our Time* (New York, HarperCollins, 1994).

Fox, R., "So . . . just what IS an MSE?", *Ministers-at-Work: The Journal for Christians in Secular Ministry* 103 (October 2007), pp. 10–18.

Fox, R., "Being MSE in Lockdown", *Ministers-at-Work: The Journal for Christians in Secular Ministry* 153 (April 2020), pp. 9–11.

Fox, R., "The view from the office window—MSE in lockdown", *Ministers-at-Work: The Journal for Christians in Secular Ministry* 154 (July 2020), pp. 4–7.

France, R. T., *Divine Government: God's Kingship in the Gospel of Mark* (London: SPCK, 1990).

Francis, J. M. M., "Some Reflections from the Perspective of Ministry in Secular Employment", in J. Davies (ed.) *God and the Marketplace: Essays on the Morality of Wealth Creation* (London: IEA, 1993), pp. 125–40.

Francis, J. M. M. and Francis, L. J., *Tentmaking: Perspectives on Self-Supporting Ministry* (Leominster: Gracewing, 1998).

Francis, J. M. M., "God as Worker: A Metaphor from Daily Life in Biblical Perspective", in R. Bisschops and J. M. M. Francis (eds), *Metaphor, Canon and Community: Jewish, Christian and Islamic Approaches* (Bern: Peter Lang, 1999), pp. 13–28.

Francis, J. M. M., "Discipleship and Vocation: Living Theology Today", *Rural Theology* 7:2 (2009), pp. 75–82.

Francis, J. M. M., "Nature Untamed: Some Reflections from Scripture", *Rural Theology* 15:1 (2017), pp. 12–21.

Francis, J. M. M., "A Reflection on MSE", *Ministers-at-Work: The Journal for Christians in Secular Ministry* 152 (January 2020), pp. 26–32.

Franklin, B., "Health and Social Care MSEs speak about the journey with COVID-19", *Ministers-at-Work: The Journal for Christians in Secular Ministry* 153 (April 2020), p. 9.

Fraser, J., "MSE—A Ministry in Sex Employment?", in *You Do What? Stories of Non-Stipendiary Ministers in the Diocese of Worcester* (2012), pp. 19–22.

Fuller, J., "Bearing Christ in Mind", in J. Fuller and P. Vaughan (eds), *Working for the Kingdom: The Story of Ministers in Secular Employment* (London: SPCK, 1986), pp. 101–8.

Gage, J., "God's gift, not priest-lite cherry-pickers", *Church Times*, 2 March 2018, p. 14.

Gage, J., "What's in a Name?", *Ministers-at-Work: The Journal for Christians in Secular Ministry* 151 (October 2019), pp. 11–18.

Gage, J., *Priests in Secular Work: Participating in the "Missio Dei"* (Durham: Sacristy Press, 2020).

Gill, R., "Theology of the Non-Stipendiary Ministry", *Theology* 80 (1977), pp. 410–13.

Godfrey, S., "A priest in the working world is a bridge between the secular (and sometimes profane) and the sacred in people's lives", in J. Fraser (ed.), *Nothing Strange: Stories of Non-Stipendiary Ministers in the Diocese of Worcestershire* 1997, pp. 28–31.

Green, P., *The Hellenistic Age: A Short History* (New York: The Modern Library, 2008).

Hacking, R., *On the Boundary: A Vision for Non-Stipendiary Ministry* (Norwich: Canterbury Press, 1990).

Handley, J., "Blessed Code: How Christian ministry might be expressed through software development", *Personal Communication*, 8 October 2020, pp. 1–5.

Handy, C., *The Second Curve: Thoughts on Reinventing Society* (London: Random House, 2015).

Hanson, K. C., "The Galilean Fishing Economy and the Jesus Tradition", *Biblical Theology Bulletin* 27 (1997), pp. 99–111.

Hardy, D., *God's Ways with the World* (Edinburgh: T. & T. Clark, 1996).

Hardy, D., *Finding the Church* (London: SCM Press, 2001).

Hartley, H-A. M., *We worked night and day that we might not burden any of you (1 Thessalonians 2.9). Aspects of the Portrayal of Work in the Letters of Paul, Late Second Temple Judaism, the Graeco-Roman World and Early Christianity*, DPhil thesis Oxford University, 2004.

Harvey, A. E., "The workman is worthy of his hire: fortunes of a proverb in the early church", *Novum Testamentum* 24 (1982), pp. 209–21.

Hatt, M., "Holding On", in P. Baelz & W. Jacob (eds), *Ministers of the Kingdom* (London: CIO Publishing, 1985), pp. 75–83.

Hengel, M., *The Pre-Christian Paul* (London: SCM Press, 1991).

Hind, J., "Varieties of Priesthood", in J. Fuller and P. Vaughan (eds), *Working for the Kingdom: The Story of Ministers in Secular Employment* (London: SPCK, 1986), pp. 88–93.

Hock, R., "Paul's Tentmaking and the Problem of His Social Class", *Journal of Biblical Literature* 97 (1978), pp. 558–62.

Hock, R., "The Workshop as a Social Setting for Paul's Missionary Preaching", *Catholic Biblical Quarterly* 41:3 (1979), pp. 438–50.

Hock, R., *The Social Context of Paul's Ministry: Tentmaking and Apostleship* (Philadelphia: Fortress Press, 1980).

Hock, R., "The Problem of Paul's Social Class: Further Reflections", in S. Porter (ed.), *Paul's World* (Leiden: E. J. Brill, 2008), pp. 7–18.

Holness, M., "The Revd. William Faull (Vet and Vicar)", *Church Times*, 28 October 1994, p. 7.

Holt, K., "Towards a Framework for Spirituality", *Ministers-at-Work: The Journal for Christians in Secular Ministry* 44 (December 1992), pp. 8–10.

Hughes, J., *The End of Work: Theological Critiques of Capitalism* (Oxford: Blackwell, 2007).

Hull, J. M., "Spiritual Development: Interpretations and Applications", *British Journal of Religious Education* 24:3 (2002), pp. 171–82.

Hurst, A., *Rendering Unto Caesar* (Worthing: Churchman Publishing, 1986).

Hurst, A., "Bridging Two Worlds", Second National Conference of Ministers in Secular Employment, Manchester, April 1986, published as a *Supplement to the Newsletter among Ministers at Work*.

Hurst, A., "Towards a Theology of Paid Employment", *Expository Times* 98 (1987), pp. 260–3.

Hurst, A., "The Pastor's Opportunities", *Expository Times* 99 (1988), pp. 100–4.

Inge, J., *A Christian Theology of Place* (Abingdon: Routledge, 2016).

Jantzen, G., "Feminism and Flourishing: Gender and Metaphor", *Feminist Theology* 18 (1995), pp. 81–101.

Jantzen, G., *Foundations of Violence* (Abingdon: Routledge, 2004).

Jasper, D., "Art and Religion in the Contemporary World", in R. Noake and N. Buxton (eds), *Religion, Society and God: Public Theology in Action* (London: SCM Press, 2014).

Jenkins, D. E., "Putting Theology to Work", *Theology* 81 (1978), pp. 114–19.

Jenkins, D. E., "Christian Faith in God", in *Still Living with Questions* (London: SCM Press, 1990), pp. 28–36.

Jenkins, T., *An Experiment in Providence: How Faith Engages with the World* (London, SPCK, 2006).

John Paul II, *Laborem Exercens* (1981).

Johnson, D., "Spirituality for Work", *Ministers-At-Work Occasional Paper* 3 (1997).

Johnson, D., "Ordained Ministers in Secular Employment", *Theology* 101 (1998), pp. 22–8.

Johnson, D., *A Ministers-At-Work Theology Resource Book* (1999), *A Chrism Publication*.

Johnson, L. T., *The Revelatory Body: Theology as Inductive Art* (Grand Rapids, MI: Eerdmans, 2015).

Johnson, P., "Making a Difference: An MSE Journey of Reflection", *Ministers-At-Work Occasional Paper* 8 (2004).

Johnson, P., *Priest of the Profane* (Beau Bassin, Mauritius: Blessed Hope Publishing, 2018).

Keighley, T., "Problems of Definition", *Ministry in Secular Employment (MSE) in the Church of England, 1960–2000: An investigation into how MSE has evolved between 1960 and 2000 and the narratives generated, to illuminate facets of the ecclesiology that have interfaced with the concurrent socio-cultural context*, PhD thesis, King's College, London, 2015, pp. 25–9.

Keighley, T., "New Ministries—New Ministers", in M. Percy, I. S. Markham, E. Percy, E. and F. Po (eds), *The Study of Ministry* (London: SPCK, 2019), pp. 420–31.

Knowles, E., "A Living Priesthood", in Fraser, J. (ed.) *Nothing Strange: Stories of Non-Stipendiary Ministers in the Diocese of Worcestershire* (1997), pp. 25–6 and updated in Fraser, J. (ed.) *You Do What? Stories of Non-Stipendiary Ministers in the Diocese of Worcester* (2012), pp. 13–15.

Kuhrt, G. (ed.), *Ministry Issues for the Church of England* (London: Church House Publishing, 2001).

Lakoff, G. and Johnson, M., *Metaphors We Live By* (Chicago: University of Chicago Press, 1980).

Lampe, G. W., "Secularisation in the New Testament and the Early Church", *Theology* 71 (1968), pp. 163–75.

Langley, R., "Non-Stipendiary Ministry in Context", in P. Baelz & W. Jacob (eds), *Ministers of the Kingdom* (London: CIO Publishing, 1985), pp. 4–15.

Larive, A., *After Sunday: A Theology of Work* (London: Continuum, 2004).

Lathem, E. C. (ed.), *The Poetry of Robert Frost* (London: Vintage, 2001).

Lave, J. and Wenger, E., *Situated Learning: Legitimate Peripheral Participation* (Cambridge: Cambridge University Press, 1991).

Lees, J., *Self-Supporting Ministry: A Practical Guide* (London: SPCK, 2018).

Levertov, D., *The Poet in the World* (New York: New Directions, 1973).

Levertov, D., "Work that Enfaiths", in *New and Selected Essays* (New York: New Directions, 1992).

Levine, A-J. and Brettler, M. Z. (eds), *The Jewish Annotated New Testament (NRSV)* (Oxford: Oxford University Press, 2011).

Lyon, P., *Church Times*, 8 March 2019, p. 56.

MacIntyre, A., *Dependent Rational Animals: Why Human Beings Need the Virtues* (London: Duckworth, 1999).

Mack, G., "Experiencing Ministry in Secular Employment", in J. M. M. Francis and L. J. Francis, *Tentmaking: Perspectives on Self-Supporting Ministry* (Leominster: Gracewing, 1998), pp. 325–8.

Mantle, J., *Britain's First Worker-Priests: Radical Ministry in a Post-War Setting* (London: SCM Press, 2000).

Mason, K., "Can a Priest ever be Part-Time?", *Crucible* (1975), pp. 21–30.

Mason, K., *Priesthood and Society* (Norwich: Canterbury Press, 1992).

Mathers, J., "A Healthy Society", in D. Willows and J. Swinton (eds), *Spiritual Dimensions of Pastoral Care: Practical Theology in a Multidisciplinary Context* (London: Jessica Kingsley Publishers, 2004), pp. 151–7.

Matthews, M., *Both Alike to Thee: The Retrieval of the Mystic Way* (London: SPCK, 2000).

Maurer, C., "Grund und Grenze apostolischer Freiheit: exegetisch-theologische Studie zu 1 Korinther 9", in *Antwort: Festschrift zum 70. Geburtstag von Karl Barth* (Zollikon-Zurich: Evangelischer Verlag, AG, 1956).

Mayne, M., *Pray, Love, Remember* (London: Darton, Longman and Todd, 2013).

McFague, S., *Speaking in Parables: A Study in Metaphor and Theology* (Philadelphia: Fortress Press, 1975).

McFague, S., *Super, Natural Christians* (Minneapolis: Fortress Press, 1997).

McFague, S., *Life Abundant* (Minneapolis: Fortress Press, 2001).

Merton, T., *Contemplative Prayer* (Garden City, NY: Doubleday Image, 1971).

Mitchell, A., "The hairdresser cutting it as a vicar", BBC News, 21 January 2020.

Moody, C., *Eccentric Ministry: Pastoral Care and Leadership in the Parish* (London: Darton, Longman and Todd, 1992).

Moore, G., *Virtue at Work: Ethics for Individuals, Managers and Organisations* (Oxford: Oxford University Press, 2017).

Murphy-O'Connor, J., *Paul: A Critical Life* (Oxford: Oxford University Press, 1996).

Murphy-O'Connor, J., *Paul: His Story* (Oxford: Oxford University Press, 2003).

Newell, J. P., *The Book of Creation: The Practice of Celtic Spirituality* (Norwich: Canterbury Press, 1999).

Noakes, K., "Word and Sacrament: Ministry of the Sacrament" in P. Baelz & W. Jacob (eds), *Ministers of the Kingdom* (London: CIO Publishing, 1985), pp. 61–5.

Nouwen, H., *The Wounded Healer* (London: Darton, Longman & Todd, 1979).

O'Donohue, J., *Anam Cara: Spiritual Wisdom from the Celtic World* (London: Bantam Books, 1999).

Oliver, M., "Franz Marc's Blue Horses", in *Devotions: The Selected Poems of Mary Oliver* (New York: Penguin, 2017).

Pacitti, D., "Clay Genesis", *Dark Angelic Mills* (Norwich, Canterbury Press 2020).

Palk, D., "God is Community", *Personal Communication*, 28 October 1999, pp. 1–10.

Patrides, C. A., (ed.), *The English Poems of George Herbert* (London: J. M. Dent, 1974).

Percy, M., *Clergy: The Origin of Species* (London: Continuum, 2006).

Percy, M., (ed. with I. S. Markham, E. Percy and F. Po), *The Study of Ministry* (London: SPCK, 2019).

Picardo, R., *Ministry Makeover: Recovering a Theology for Bi-Vocational Service in the Church* (Eugene, OR: Wipf & Stock, 2015).

Pickering, W. S. F., "The Parish Priest and the Secular World", *Theology* 77 (1974), pp. 572–8.

Pitt, T., "Spirituality and the MSE", *Ministers-at-Work: The Journal for Christians in Secular Ministry* 33 (1990), pp. 9–11.

Powell, M., "Playing Cards: Making Connections", *Personal Communication*, 24 October 1999, pp. 1–10.

Pring, R., "Markets, Education and Catholic Schools", in T. H. McLaughlin, J. O'Keefe and B. O'Keeffe (eds), *The Contemporary Catholic School: Context, Identity and Diversity* (London, Falmer Press, 1996).

Pritchard, J., "Ministry in Secular Employment: The Original Fresh Expression", *Ministers-at-Work: The Journal for Christians in Secular Ministry* 108 (2009), pp. 16–19.

Rahner K., *Faith in a Wintry Season* (New York: Crossroad, 1990).

Ramsey, M., *The Christian Priest Today* revised edition (London: SPCK, 1985).

Ranken, M., "A Theology for the Priest at Work", *Theology* 85 (1982), pp. 108–13.

Ranken, M., "Style and Community" in J. Fuller and P. Vaughan (eds), *Working for the Kingdom* (London: SPCK, 1986), pp. 60–7.

Ranken, M., "Ministry in Secular Employment and the Church's Mission", in *Ordained Ministry in Secular Employment: Reflections on the History and Theology*, ACCM Occasional Paper, 31 February 1989, pp. 7–24.

Ranken, M., "Mile in My Moccasins", *Guildford Cathedral Papers* (Autumn 1990).

Raven, C. E., *Science, Religion and the Future* (Cambridge: Cambridge University Press, 2008).

Rayner, K., *Ordained Ministry in Secular Employment: Reflections on the History and Theology*, ACCM Occasional Paper 31 (1989), pp. 25–43.

Rayner, M., "Editorial", *Ministers-At-Work: The Journal for Christians in Secular Ministry* 118 (July/October 2011), pp. 2–7.

Reindorp, J., *Equipping Christians at Work* (London: London Industrial Christian Fellowship, 2000).

Robinson, J. A. T., *On Being the Church in the World* (London: SCM Press, 1964).

Robson, J., "How to Make a Prophet at Work" in J. Fuller and P. Vaughan (eds), *Working for the Kingdom* (London: SPCK, 1986), pp. 79–88.

Rowe, J., "Communication Across Class Barriers", in C. Lind and T. Brown (eds), *Justice As Mission: An Agenda For The Church* (Burlington, Ontario: Trinity Press, 1985).

Rodwell, J., *Blessings in Disguise*, Keynote Address to the Second National Conference of Ministers in Secular Employment, Manchester, April 1986, published as *A Supplement to the Newsletter among Ministers at Work*, and in *Southwell & Oxford Papers on Contemporary Society* (August 1987).

Rodwell, J., "Well, bless me", in J. Novell (ed.), *Reflections on Non-Stipendiary Ministry* (Diocese of Blackburn, 2003), pp. 17–19.

Russell, A., *The Clerical Profession* (London: SPCK, 1980).

Sacks, J., *The Home We Build Together: Recreating Society* (London: Continuum, 2007).

Saunders, B., "Scrutiny of non-stipendiaries put in hand", *Church Times*, 26 January 1990.

Sawle, M., in J. Novell (ed.), *Reflections on Non-Stipendiary Ministry*, (Diocese of Blackburn, 2003), pp. 20–5.

Skinner, J., "Not Quite Kosher", *Personal Communication*, 1 October 1999, pp. 1–8.

Soelle, D., *The Silent Cry: Mysticism and Resistance* (Minneapolis: Fortress Press, 2001).

Sweeney, J., *From Story to Policy: Social Inclusion, Empowerment and the Churches* (Cambridge: Von Hügel Institute, 2001).

Taylor, B. B., *An Altar in the World* (Norwich: Canterbury Press, 2009).

Theissen, G., *The Social Setting of Pauline Christianity* (Edinburgh: T. &. T. Clark, 1982).

Thomas, R. S., *Collected Poems 1945–1990* (London, Phoenix, 1993).

Thompson-McCausland, M., *Personal Communication*, 5 September 1999, pp. 1–6.

Thornton, M., "The Ministry of Prayer", in P. Baelz & W. Jacob (eds), *Ministers of the Kingdom* (London: CIO Publishing, 1985), pp. 66–74.

Tiller, J., *A Strategy for the Church's Ministry* (London: CIO, 1983).

Tripp, K., *Personal Communication*, 25 February 2019, pp. 1–2.

Trivasse, M., "Where is 'the Touching Place' now?", *Ministers-at-Work: The Journal for Christians in Secular Ministry* 154 (July 2020), pp. 16–18.

Turnbull, M., *Setting the Compass: An Address to the Diocese of Durham* (2000).

Van Sloten, J., *Every Job a Parable* (London: Hodder & Stoughton, 2017).

Vaughan, P., "Speaking for Themselves", in P. Baelz & W. Jacob (eds), *Ministers of the Kingdom* (London: CIO Publishing, 1985), pp. 16–31.

Vaughan, P., "Evidence from Practitioners", in J. Fuller and P. Vaughan (eds), *Working for the Kingdom* (London: SPCK, 1986), pp. 9–54.

Vaughan, P., "An Historical Perspective on Ministers in Secular Employment", in J. Fuller and P. Vaughan (eds), *Working for the Kingdom* (London: SPCK, 1986), pp. 117–87.

Vaughan, P., *Non-Stipendiary Ministry in the Church of England: The History of the Development of an Idea* (San Francisco: Edwin Mellen Press, 1990).

Vest, N., *Friend of the Soul: A Benedictine Spirituality of Work* (Cowley, MA: Cowley Publications, 1997).

Voillaume, R., *Brothers of Men: Letters to the Petits Frères* (London: Darton, Longman & Todd, 1966).

Wakefield, G. S., *A Dictionary of Christian Spirituality* (London: SCM Press, 1983).

Walsh, C., *Frequencies of God: Walking through Advent with R. S. Thomas* (Norwich, Canterbury Press, 2020).

Watson, P., *Personal Communication*, 19 November 1999, pp. 1–13.

Wedgeworth, M., "Priesthood and Management: A Contradiction in Terms?", in Novell, J. (ed.), *Reflections on Non-Stipendiary Ministry* (Diocese of Blackburn, 2003), pp. 37–40.

Weil, S., *Letter to a Priest* (Abingdon: Routledge, 2002).

Whipp, M. J., *Speaking of Faith at Work: Towards a Trinitarian Hermenuetic*, PhD thesis, Glasgow University, 2008.

White, W., "Some Personal Thoughts from Furlough", *Ministers-at-Work: The Journal for Christians in Secular Ministry* 154 (July 2020), pp. 13–14.

Wieseltier, L., *Kaddish* (New York: Pan, 2000).

Williams, H., "Programmers are urged to adopt good habits: Software firm pastes the Rule of St Benedict into its Code of Conduct", *Church Times*, 26 October 2018, p. 2.

Williams, R., "Ordained Ministry in the Church", *Ministers-at-Work: The Journal for Christians in Secular Ministry* 42 (1992), pp. 10–11.

Williams, R., *Open to Judgement: Sermons and Addresses* (London: Darton, Longman and Todd, 1994).

Williams R., *Anglican Identities* (London: Darton, Longman and Todd, 2004).

Williams, R., "The Christian Priest Today", in D. Dales, J. Habgood, G. Rowell, R. Williams (eds), *Glory Descending: Michael Ramsey and his Writings* (Norwich: Canterbury Press, 2005), pp.163–75.

Williams, R., *Grace and Necessity: Reflections on Art and Love* (London: Continuum, 2005).

Williams, R., *Being Human: Bodies, Minds, Persons* (London: SPCK, 2018).

Williams, R., *Luminaries: Twenty Lives that Illuminate the Christian Way* (London: SPCK, 2019).

Williamson, H., "Clocking on: the world of the worker priest", *Church Times*, 6 September 2019, pp. 20–1

Wragg, T., "Bureaucracy", *Guardian E Supplement*, 15 November 2005, pp. 1–2.

Wright, N. T., *Paul: A Biography* (London: SPCK, 2019).

Yore, S., *The Mystic Way in Postmodernity: Transcending Theological Boundaries in the Writings of Iris Murdoch, Denise Levertov and Annie Dillard* (Bern: Peter Lang, 2009).

Notes

Quoted by Lionel Blue in *Best of Blue* (London: Continuum, 2006), p. 50.

[2] See Mike Rayner's "Editorial", *Ministers-At-Work: The Journal for Christians in Secular Ministry* 118 (July/October 2011), pp. 2–7, and a preference for a description as "whole-life ministers".

[3] See the wide-ranging collection of essays in M. Percy, E. Percy, I. S. Markham and F. Po (eds), *The Study of Ministry* (London: SPCK, 2019).

[4] For an exploration of some of these consequences, see V. Donovan, *Christianity Rediscovered* (London: SCM Press, 2001).

[5] See M. Ramsey, *The Christian Priest Today* (London: SPCK, 1985) (revised edition), pp. 13–14.

[6] J. Rodwell, "Well, bless me", in J. Novell, *Reflections on Non-Stipendiary Ministry* (Diocese of Blackburn, 2003), p. 17.

[7] See most recently J. Gage, *Priests in Secular Work: Participating in the "Missio Dei"* (Durham: Sacristy Press, 2020).

[8] For a similar story of unemployment see E. Knowles, "A Living Priesthood", in J. Fraser (ed.), *Nothing Strange: Stories of Non-Stipendiary Ministers in the Diocese of Worcestershire* (1997), pp. 25–6 and "A Living Priesthood Part 2" in J. Fraser (ed.), *You Do What? Stories of Non-Stipendiary Ministers in the Diocese of Worcester* (2012), pp. 13–15.

[9] J. M. M. Francis and L. J. Francis, *Tentmaking. Perspectives on Self-Supporting Ministry* (Leominster: Gracewing, 1998). A helpful definition of SSM is provided by R. Hacking in *On the Boundary: A Vision for Non-Stipendiary Ministry* (Norwich: Canterbury Press, 1990). SSMs are "those who seek, without any remuneration from the church, to exercise a full-time ministry to which they have been ordained by the church, often whilst continuing in their 'secular jobs'" (p. 20). Notably, the phrase "often whilst continuing in their secular jobs" belongs within the expression of what "a full-time ministry" is. A shorter definition is: "A representative sign of the presence in the world of the mystery of God." P. Baelz, "Ministers of the Kingdom", in P. Baelz & W.

133

Jacob (eds), *Ministers of the Kingdom* (London: CIO Publishing 1985), p. 37. Also Tom Keighley, "Problems of Definition", pp. 25–9 in *Ministry in Secular Employment (MSE) in the Church of England, 1960–2000. An investigation into how MSE has evolved between 1960 and 2000 and the narratives generated, to illuminate facets of the ecclesiology that have interfaced with the concurrent socio-cultural context.* PhD thesis, King's College, London, 2015. For a very succinct but helpful outline of the history of MSE in modern times see C. Brown, "A Brief History of the Development of Non-Stipendiary Ministry and some Commentary on the Current Situation" in *On the Boundary: Reflections on Non-Stipendiary Ministry* (Diocese of Chelmsford, 2002), pp. 4–7. For a good overview of the different expressions of Self-Supporting Ministry see M. Ranken, "Ministry in Secular Employment and the Church's Mission" in *Ordained Ministry in Secular Employment: Reflections on the History and Theology*, ACCM Occasional Paper 31, February 1989, pp. 7–24. And T. Keighley, "New Ministries—New Ministers" in *The Study of Ministry*, pp. 420–31. See also J. M. M. Francis, "A Reflection on MSE", *Ministers-at-Work: The Journal for Christians in Secular Ministry* 152 (January 2020), pp. 26–32.

[10] R. Allen, "The Case for Voluntary Clergy: an Anglican Problem", *The Interpreter* (July 1922), pp. 314ff.

[11] So, rightly, M. Austin in *Working for the Kingdom*, p. 115. See also P. Baelz, *Ministers of the Kingdom*, pp. 37ff.

[12] Hacking, *On the Boundary*, pp. 83–4.

[13] It is perhaps worth noting here the etymological link in Old English between *hal* (health) and *halig* (holy).

[14] A theme especially of Michael Ranken. John Tiller summarily dismissed this idea of priesthood. But for a trenchant reply see J. Rodwell, *Blessings in Disguise*, Keynote Address to the Second National Conference of Ministers in Secular Employment, Manchester, April 1986, published as a *Supplement to the Newsletter among Ministers at Work*, and in *Southwell & Oxford Papers on Contemporary Society*, August 1987. If Michael Ramsey's understanding of priesthood is an entering the sanctuary with the people on one's heart, this would include the context of creation in which people are set. Accordingly, one should not distinguish so easily or sharply between a care for people and the material nature of life.

[15] See J. Van Sloten, *Every Job a Parable* (London: Hodder & Stoughton, 2017).

16 See J. Lees, *Self-Supporting Ministry: A Practical Guide* (London: SPCK, 2018),
    pp. 74–5. See also D. Johnson, "Ordained Ministers in Secular Employment"
    Theology 101 (January 1998), pp. 22–8.

17 Marcus Thompson-McCausland, *Personal Communication*, 5 September
    1999, pp. 2–3, 6.

18 See L. Erlander, *Faith in the World of Work: On the Theology of Work as Lived
    by the French Worker-Priests and British Industrial Mission* (Uppsala: Uppsala
    University, 1991), pp. 155ff.

19 To be "alongside those to whom one ministers, to sit where they sit and to
    speak the language they speak", cited in John Mantle, *Britain's First Worker-
    Priests: Radical Ministry in a Post-War Setting* (London: SCM Press, 2000),
    p. 223. For a profile of contemporary worker-priests and a comparison with
    the first English worker-priests see H. Williamson, "Clocking on: the world
    of the worker-priest", *Church Times*, 6 September 2019, pp. 20–1.

20 See G. Kuhrt (ed.), *Ministry Issues for the Church of England* (London: Church
    House Publishing, 2001), pp. 221ff.

21 J. Mantle, *Britain's First Worker-Priests*, pp. 269–70. See also J. Rowe,
    "Communication Across Class Barriers", in C. Lind and T. Brown (eds),
    Justice As Mission: An Agenda For The Church (Burlington, Ontario: Trinity
    Press, 1985), pp. 35–40. Rowe notes emphatically that worker-priests are not
    about bridging the Church and the world of work but overcoming a class
    barrier. He points out what is at stake: "What can it mean to be a priest who
    cannot either in fact or in conscience lead the people around him toward the
    worshipping community? And what can it mean to be a workman who turns
    away from the locus of the Gospel—the common herd and its struggles—
    to join with a specialist society in saying its prayers? . . . But these are not
    two sides of his life—they are two polarities" (p. 40). These words remain a
    challenge. To be fair, however, it is not just a worker-priest that knows this.
    It is also the experience of many stipendiary and MSE deacons and priests,
    and many in the Church generally, all things considered.

22 *Stranger in the Wings: A Report on Local Non-Stipendiary Ministry* (London:
    Church House Publishing, 1999), pp. 34–5.

23 Ibid. p. 51.

24 Ibid. p. 57.

25 See Michael Mayne: "Priesthood expresses itself in different roles, but if the
    priest becomes the role, where there is nothing left that is not the role" then

something is lost, "for if you identify solely with your role it can begin to destroy your humanity, and you may even become a dehumanizing force within the community". M. Mayne, *Pray, Love, Remember* (London: Darton, Longman and Todd, 2013), p. 43. "Primarily I am a human being and only remain a priest because . . . this seems a good way of being human" (citing Gerard Hughes, ibid. p. 43). On role and priesthood see K. Mason, "Can a Priest ever be Part–Time?" *Crucible* (January–March 1975), pp. 21–30 esp. pp. 24ff.

26   See Chapter 5.

27   See J. Mantle, *Britain's First Worker-Priests*, p. 74. See also generally L. Erlander, *Faith in the World of Work.*

28   R. T. France, *Divine Government: God's Kingship in the Gospel of Mark* (London: SPCK, 1990), p. 13.

29   J. Fuller and P. Vaughan (eds), *Working for the Kingdom: The Story of Ministers in Secular Employment* (London: SPCK, 1986). Whilst it antedates the ordination of women (in the Church of England), the book provides a valuable reflection on the diversity of MSE experience, with accompanying (often trenchant) assessment by a group of contributors who interact in some detail with the evidence of the stories. The book is a distillation of reflections from a larger archive of unpublished material. For a general perspective see *Towards a Theology of Ministry in Secular Employment* (Diocese of Southwark, 1997). See also the short stories in J. Lees, *Self-Supporting Ministry: A Practical Guide.*

30   See D. Davies, "Person, Power and Priesthoods", in *Working for the Kingdom*, pp. 93–101, esp. pp. 97–8. See also K. Mason, *Priesthood and Society* (Norwich: Canterbury Press, 1992), especially chapter 1 "The Necessity of Priesthood".

31   Paul Watson, *Personal Communication*, 19 November 1999, pp. 6, 11.

32   We should note John Rodwell's objection to the metaphor of bridge which supposes a gap between world and Church, whereas "wherever we are, God is there already, waiting to be revealed". "Well, bless me", *Reflections on Non-Stipendiary Ministry*, ed. J. Novell, pp. 17–19. (For a different kind of gap (of class) see J. Rowe note 21 above.) In all likelihood, MSE is for some a misnomer, since there is no such thing (*au fond*) as sacred and secular employment. Nevertheless, the metaphor of bridge remains useful for many MSEs. See S. Godfrey, "A priest in the working world is a bridge between the secular (and sometimes profane) and the sacred in people's lives", *Nothing*

Strange: Stories of Non-Stipendiary Ministers in the Diocese of Worcestershire, ed. J. Fraser (1997), pp. 28–31. Also Jane Fraser, "The MSE is often seen as a bridge between the sacred world of the church and the secular world of work; a part of each but not belonging entirely to each. I would endorse that but see the ministry I've been given as increasingly complex." *You Do What? Stories of Non-Stipendiary Ministers in the Diocese of Worcester*, (2012), pp. 19–22, at p. 22. See also note 57. More generally, it is worthwhile noting how dissonance between contexts, such as is debated in situated learning theory, is not something that emerges very often in MSE awareness. See Jean Lave and Etienne Wenger, *Situated Learning: Legitimate Peripheral Participation* (Cambridge: Cambridge University Press, 1991). This says something about the broadly holistic vision that MSEs hold.

[33] See J. Hind, "Varieties of Priesthood", in *Working for the Kingdom*, pp. 88–93, especially pp. 90, 93.

[34] See J. Fuller, "Bearing Christ in Mind", in *Working for the Kingdom*, pp. 101–8, especially pp. 104–5.

[35] "The cry of Jerusalem is the cry of creation groaning and travailing even until now, waiting for the revelation of the sons and daughters of God. 'Preach the gospel to all creation' Christ said. Are we only now beginning to understand what he meant? I believe the unwritten melody that haunts this book ever so faintly, the new song waiting to be sung in place of the hymn of salvation, is simply the song of creation. To move away from the theology of salvation to the theology of creation may be the task of our time." V. Donovan, *Christianity Rediscovered*, Preface to the Second Edition, p. xx.

[36] Mantle, *Britain's First Worker-Priests*, p. 74.

[37] So J. Davis, "Lay and Ordained in the Workplace", in *Working for the Kingdom*, pp. 74–9, especially p. 78. Davis continues: "The only clear distinction between MSEs and lay colleagues at work is in the area of personal pastoral ministry". See further note 148.

[38] See J. M. M. Francis, "Discipleship and Vocation: Living Theology Today", *Rural Theology* 7:2 (2009), pp. 75–82. As good a definition of vocation is this: "Wilberforce believed politics was a vocation because he saw politics as always opening out beyond itself." R. Williams, *Luminaries: Twenty Lives that Illuminate the Christian Way* (London: SPCK, 2019) p. 87.

[39] See the helpful observations of J. Lees, *Self-Supporting Ministry: A Practical Guide*, pp. 78–9, and also Jenny Gage, pp. 20–1 in that same book.

40   See A. Hurst, "The Pastor's Opportunities", *Expository Times* 99 (1988), pp. 100–4, for an outline of the variety of circumstances MSEs can encounter. See also P. Vaughan, "Speaking for Themselves", in P. Baelz & W. Jacob (eds), *Ministers of the Kingdom*, pp. 16–31; P. Vaughan, "Evidence from Practitioners", in *Working for the Kingdom*, pp. 9–54; J. Lees, *Self-Supporting Ministry: A Practical Guide* provides, chapter by chapter, an "SSM in Practice" case study.

41   Despite criticism in *Working for the Kingdom* of a lack of prophetic action amongst MSEs (pages 77–78), some of the MSE stories do indicate what might be considered as prophetic concern. See Jill Robson, "How to Make a Prophet at Work", *Working for the Kingdom* pp. 79–88. It is best not to make too sharp a distinction between the models of prophet and servant, not least where this is informed by the ministry of Jesus. See the stories of MSEs themselves in Lees, *Self-Supporting Ministry: A Practical Guide*. See also Bishop Michael Turnbull's statement in an essay to the Diocese of Durham: "Ministers in secular employment play a prophetic part in a priesthood which is as valid in the workplace as in the local church" (*Setting the Compass* (2000), p. 13); see also I. Cundy "Ministry of the Word", in Baelz and Jacob (eds), *Ministers of the Kingdom*, p. 59. Paul Watson, *Personal Communication*, p. 12 says: "My commitment is to justice arising from my understanding of the Christian Gospel, and my belief in the need to act consistently has driven me on several occasions to take a prophetic role with the College authorities . . . those in leadership roles must be accountable, and I have both the right and the duty to question their perception of the truth." Deirdre Palk says: "I am an ambassador for the "Kingdom" issues of health and safety, care and justice; my message is that people matter more than structures and profits, but also that structures and profits can go hand in hand with care for people." "God is Community", *Personal Communication*, 28 October 1999, p. 7.

42   Davies in *Working for the Kingdom*, pp. 100–1.

43   See M. Matthews, *Both Alike to Thee: The Retrieval of the Mystic Way* (London: SPCK, 2000).

44   Anthea Mitchell BBC News item "The hairdresser cutting it as a vicar", 21 January 2020. See also the Revd. Gary Dundas, "Sausages and sermons on offer as butcher becomes priest", BBC News Derby, 5 November 2011: "The customers who know me think it's lovely. I get asked for prayers quite a lot and it's very special."

45 R. Williams, *Open to Judgement: Sermons and Addresses* (London: Darton, Longman and Todd, 1994), p. 182.

46 P. Vaughan, "An Historical Perspective on Ministers in Secular Employment", in Fuller and Vaughan (eds), *Working for the Kingdom*, pp. 117–87. See also A. Russell, *The Clerical Profession* (London: SPCK, 1980), p. 249; M. Percy, *Clergy: The Origin of Species* (London: Continuum, 2006), pp. 26–8.

47 On this see particularly Chapters 3 and 4. As David E. Jenkins put it: "There is a church of God, certainly, but not a God of the church". The philosopher and novelist Iris Murdoch especially liked Philippians 4:8, "Whatsoever things are true, whatsoever things are honourable, whatsoever things are just, whatsoever things are pure, whatsoever things are lovely, whatsoever things are of good report . . . think on these things", in her conviction that we must strive for the Good as the moral basis of society. ("Literature and Philosophy: A Conversation with Bryan Magee", in P. Conradi (ed.), *Iris Murdoch: Existentialists and Mystics* (London: Penguin, 1997). p. 5.

48 The saying at Luke 10:7 and Matthew 10:10b (cf. 1 Timothy 5:18 and alluded to by Paul in 1 Corinthians 9:7,14) reflects an entitlement to hospitality, not payment. See Excursus.

49 Radio Leeds programme "One on One", 8 January 2013. See also the Diocese of Leeds' e-newsletter <http://www.leeds.anglican.org/news/hundreds-fill-leeds-minster-funeral-much-loved-busker-jonny-walker>, accessed 13 July 2020, for a service held in Leeds Minster. "Jonny was a devoted father, street entertainer, campaigner, professional musician and activist." He was a patron of "Musical Keys", a charity working to develop the gifts of young people with special needs through music. See also "Flute Player Busking for Charity" about Nicola Miriams busking in different locations across the country for charitable causes. "The busking challenge started last December in Sidmouth, Devon", *Durham Advertiser*, 11 October 2018, p. 5.

50 Type "Science/Maths Busking" into a search engine to find a range of initiatives to promote science and maths.

51 G. Lakoff and M. Johnson point out (p. 13) that "metaphorical structuring . . . is partial not total. If it were total, one concept would actually *be* the other, not merely be understood in terms of it. For example, 'life is a journey' Thus, part of a metaphorical concept does not and cannot fit. On the other hand, metaphorical concepts can be extended beyond the range of ordinary literal ways of thinking and talking into the range of what is called figurative, poetic,

colourful, or fanciful thought and language." G. Lakoff and M. Johnson, *Metaphors We Live By* (Chicago: University of Chicago Press, 1980).

[52] "The correct criterion to employ in certain debates, e.g. those of literary criticism, is (usually) not one of correctness/incorrectness, or right/wrong, but one of appropriateness." E. Borg, "An Expedition Abroad: Metaphor, Thought and Reporting", *Midwest Studies in Philosophy* 25:1 (August 2001), 227–48, p. 240.

[53] R. Fagles, *Homer, The Odyssey* (New York: Penguin, 1996), pp. 14ff.

[54] Daniel Barenboim in his Reith Lectures for 2006 says: "The New Testament says 'in the beginning was the Word', and Goethe says 'in the beginning was the deed'. But the musician says 'in the beginning was the silence'". See also S. C. Barton, "New Testament Interpretation as Performance", *Scottish Journal of Theology* 52:2 (1999), pp. 179–208.

[55] Mason, *Priesthood and Society*, pp. 52–3 (written at a time before the ordination of women). One is reminded of Rahere the Augustinian monk and musician, herald and jester at the court of Henry I. In the twelfth century the same person was often a musician and a herald. He was Founder of the Priory of the Hospital of St. Bartholomew in London in 1123. Above the altar in the chapel is a triptych window, and in the right hand panel is the kneeling figure of Rahere wearing his black Augustinian habit with one leg showing his motley jester's stockings. I am indebted to Margaret Joachim, MSE and Area Director of Ordinands, Diocese of London, for mentioning this.

[56] "Priests of the world" as James Quinn describes the Church in mission in his hymn "Forth in the peace of Christ we go".

[57] See Mack, "The minister in secular employment is the fool on the edge of both worlds who must retain, at all costs, the freedom to cross the boundaries and often to live in the no-man's land in between. Such a minister, and especially such a deacon, must also be a bridge: firmly anchored to both ends and prepared to be walked over." "Experiencing Ministry in Secular Employment", in J. M. M. Francis and L. J. Francis (eds), *Tentmaking: Perspectives on Self-Supporting Ministry*, pp. 325–8, p. 326; also cited in J. Lees, *Self-Supporting Ministry: A Practical Guide*, p. 44.

[58] Bryony Franklin, "Health and Social Care MSEs speak about the journey with COVID-19", *Ministers-at-Work: The Journal for Christians in Secular Ministry* 153 (April 2020), p. 9.

[59] Baelz, *Ministers of the Kingdom*, p. 36.

[60] Robert Fox, "The view from the office window—MSE in lockdown", *Ministers-at-Work: The Journal for Christians in Secular Ministry* 154 (July 2020), pp. 4–7, especially pp. 5, 7.

[61] Baelz, *Ministers of the Kingdom*, pp. 34–5.

[62] See R. Williams, *Grace and Necessity: Reflections on Art and Love* (London: Continuum, 2005), pp. 56ff.

[63] See C. Handy, *The Second Curve: Thoughts on Reinventing Society* (London: Random House, 2015), in which the author characterizes the second curve as a capacity in a time of rapid change to think critically and imaginatively.

[64] Phil Aspinall, "Condemned to Insecurity?", *Ministers-at-Work: The Journal for Christians in Secular Ministry* 143 (October 2017), pp. 25–30, especially p. 27.

[65] See Mantle, *Britain's First Worker-Priests*, p. 264ff., and J. Rowe, "Communication Across Class Barriers".

[66] Wendy White, "Some Personal Thoughts from Furlough", *Ministers-at-Work* 154 (July 2020), pp. 13–14.

[67] See below, Chapter 6 on MSE and Spirituality.

[68] Keith Tripp, *Personal Communication*, 25 February 2019, p. 1.

[69] Williams, *Open to Judgement*, pp. 16–17.

[70] R. Williams: " . . . in the ministerial life, there must be skill and willingness and space for at least three things. The priest has to be free to be a lookout, an interpreter, and what I can best call a weaver." "The Christian Priest Today", in D. Dales, J. Habgood, G. Rowell and R. Williams (eds), *Glory Descending: Michael Ramsey and his Writings* (Norwich: Canterbury Press, 2005), pp. 166ff.

[71] Cf. the last stanza of Charlotte Elliott's hymn *Just as I am*:

Just as I am, of that free love
The breadth, length, depth, and height to prove.

[72] D. Jasper, "Art and Religion in the Contemporary World", in R. Noake and N. Buxton (eds), *Religion, Society and God: Public Theology in Action* (London: SCM Press, 2014) pp. 66–80, especially p. 73. On the desire to make something beautiful as that of God within each of us see Mary Oliver, "Franz Marc's Blue Horses", in *Devotions: The Selected Poems of Mary Oliver* (New York: Penguin, 2017), p. 21.

[73] C. Cocksworth and R. Brown, *Being a Priest Today* (Norwich: Canterbury Press, 2nd edition, 2006), pp. 5–6.

[74] This probably goes back to the Reformation and the lack of clarity (in Luther) about what exactly the priesthood of all believers might mean. See K. Mason, *Priesthood and Society*, pp. 127ff.

[75] For Paul "bodies" means (by and large) the self in both its spiritual and physical aspects—the embodied self, as we might say, i.e. the self in the nexus of life and relationships in the world around us.

[76] *The Mission and Ministry of the Whole Church: Biblical, Theological and Contemporary Perspectives*, GS Misc.854 (London: Church House Publishing, 2007).

[77] Ibid. pp. 56ff.

[78] On Michael Ramsey, in R. Williams, *Anglican Identities* (London: Darton, Longman and Todd, 2004) pp. 94–5.

[79] See M. Bourke, "The Theology of Non-Stipendiary Ministry", *Theology* 84 (1981), pp. 177–82. In 1974, W. S. F. Pickering (a sociologist and MSE) drew attention to the dynamic between social context and institutions. "The exercise of ministry can never be confined to institutional occasions or opportunities. In one sense, ministry is without social restriction. But, on the other hand, institutional channels are the general means of communication. They have been established and are recognised as such by participants." He makes an argument for an institutional permissiveness on the part of the Church where "in our allegedly secularised society, folk religion lingers on, is tenacious, and almost thrives". "The Parish Priest and the Secular World", *Theology* 77 (1974), pp. 572–8.

[80] See *The Mission and Ministry of the Whole Church* (London: CIO, 2007).

[81] Donovan, *Christianity Rediscovered*, p. 130.

[82] See Mantle, *Britain's First Worker-Priests*, p. 74.

[83] See Vaughan, "Evidence from Practitioners", pp. 31–44 in Fuller and Vaughan *Working for the Kingdom*. See also Vaughan, "Speaking for Themselves", in *Ministers of the Kingdom*, pp. 16ff.

[84] See Cocksworth and Brown, *Being a Priest Today*, p. 26; P. Johnson, *Priest of the Profane* (Beau Bassin, Mauritius: Blessed Hope Publishing, 2018), pp. 21–2. See also Martineau, *The Office and Work of a Priest*: priesthood is to be "alongside those to whom one ministers, to sit where they sit and to speak the language they speak", cited in Mantle, *Britain's First Worker-Priests*, p. 223.

85 Mantle, *Britain's First Worker-Priests*, pp. 108ff.

86 Mantle, *Britain's First Worker-Priests*, pp. 72, 74ff., 135.

87 Williams, *Anglican Identities*, pp. 87–8. See also Mike Hatt, "Holding On", *Ministers of the Kingdom*, pp. 75–83.

88 See also Vaughan, "Speaking for Themselves", in *Ministers of the Kingdom*, pp. 16–31, particularly the six forms listed on pp. 30–1, and Vaughan, "Evidence from Practitioners", in Fuller and Vaughan, *Working for the Kingdom*, pp. 20ff. Also Ian Bunting, *Models of Ministry: Managing the Church Today*, Grove Pastoral Series 54 (Cambridge: Grove Books, 1996).

89 For an eloquent and thorough statement of this see R. Fox, "So . . . just what IS an MSE?", *Ministers-at-Work: The Journal for Christians in Secular Ministry* 103 (October 2007), pp. 10–18.

90 See Williams, "The Christian Priest Today", pp. 163–75. See also Mason, "Can a Priest ever be Part-Time?" "Their desire is not so much that among the workers there should be priests, in the interest of mission to the workers, as that some priests should be workers for the enrichment of the priesthood, and the indirect pastoral gains that should follow from that." (p. 23). A similar statement is found amongst the worker-priest literature. (One notes in this article the judiciously chosen term of "priest-workers", as described by the then Chapter in the Diocese of Southwark. So also A. Hurst, *Rendering unto Caesar* (Worthing: Churchman Publishing, 1986), Chapter 8 "Ordained Ministry in the Workplace". See also J. Gage, "What's in a Name?", *Ministers-at-Work: The Journal for Christians in Secular Ministry* 151 (October 2019), pp. 11–18 for the description "priests in secular work—PSW".

91 From a story of Rabbi Elimelekh of Lizhensk: " . . . Those who work something because God gives them the power to do it know of no whence and no how, and the wonder which arises out of their doing overwhelms them themselves." M. Buber, *Tales of the Hasidim: The Early Masters* (New York: Schocken Books, 1975), pp. 262–3. See also D. Levertov, *Collected Earlier Poems 1940–1960* (New York: New Directions, 1979), who cites this for her poem "Notes of a Scale iv", pp. 104–5.

92 See C. G. Clark, "A Rumour of Priests", *Theology* 92 (1989), pp. 20–5. See also note 25 above.

93 Deirdre Palk, "God is Community", *Personal Communication*, p. 5.

94 See Cundy, "Ministry of the Word", pp. 55–6, and Noakes, "Word and Sacrament" in Baelz and Jacob, *Ministers of the Kingdom*, pp. 64ff.

[95] See John Paul II, *Laborem Exercens* (1981). Also Hurst, *Rendering Unto Caesar*, pp. 20ff. The poet Robert Frost reflects on these themes in his poem "Two Tramps in Mud Time", *The Poetry of Robert Frost*, ed. E. Connery Lathem (London: Vintage, 2001), pp. 275–7, written after two casual labour lumberjacks happened on his farm in New Hampshire while he was cutting wood. He meditates on how work both as necessity to earn a living and as personal fulfilment might be as one.

[96] See J. M. M. Francis, "Discipleship and Vocation", *Rural Theology* 17:2 (2009), pp. 75–82. Also J. Lees, *Self-Supporting Ministry: A Practical Guide*, Chapter 5 "Called to the Margins", pp. 44–53. The Church might do more to recognize that the workplace can be a tough place to be. "There's so much more to be done to look after employees. The Rise of 'Presenteeism' in the Workplace", BBC News Business, 14 April 2019.

[97] See T. Jenkins, "Community and Vocation", in *An Experiment in Providence: How Faith Engages with the World* (London: SPCK, 2006), pp. 14–24.

[98] See Rabbi J. Sacks, *The Home We Build Together: Recreating Society* (London: Continuum, 2007).

[99] See *Glory Descending: Michael Ramsey and his Writings*, p. 79. Petr Eben, Czech composer (who survived Buchenwald, and persecution under the Communist regime for refusing to join the Party and for continuing to attend church): "Perhaps the most urgent task of art is to praise, otherwise the stones would cry out."

[100] Evident in some of the art of Marc Chagall. Cf. Leon Wieseltier, *Kaddish* (London: Pan, 2000). See also Diane Pacitti, "Clay Genesis", *Dark Angelic Mills* (Norwich: Canterbury Press, 2020), pp. 22–3.

[101] Simone Weil, *Letter to a Priest* (Routledge: Abingdon, 2002), p. 43.

[102] See J. M. M. Francis, "Nature Untamed: Some Reflections from Scripture", *Rural Theology* 15:1 (2017), pp. 12–21.

[103] See *The English Poems of George Herbert*, ed. C. A. Patrides (London: J. M. Dent, 1974), pp. 70–1. The lines are: " . . . The six-daies world-transposing in an houre,
A kinde of tune, which all things heare and fear; . . . "
"In these lines: 'transposing' resonates alliteratively with 'tune' as a musical term indicating sounds reproduced at another pitch from that at which they were originally written. The image is made explicit in the next line; its centrality was recognized by Vaughan: 'Prayer is/The world in tune'

("*The Morning-watch*", 18–19)." (Patrides, footnote 7 on p. 71). The musical metaphor of transposition conveys both the idea of the sovereign glory of God that pervades creation and therefore does not inherently belong to it, and the creativity of humankind in the reflection of this glory (supremely as the creative work of prayer, and life as prayer cf. the phrase "*laborare est orare*"), that is not ours but God's. In this surely, as Daniel Barenboim has claimed (The Reith Lectures for 2006), music is a metaphor for life.

[104] Weil, *Letter to a Priest*, p. 45. See also Carys Walsh, "The Coming" in *Frequencies of God: Walking through Advent with R. S. Thomas* (Norwich: Canterbury Press, 2020), pp. 3–6.

[105] Paul speaks of "new" as "*kainé*", i.e. it is not new as another creation but creation renewed. So also at John 1:14 it is clear that the Incarnation is the outcome of the prior creative work of God through the Word in 1:1. See also Hacking, *On the Boundary*, Chapters 3 (the boundary between Church and Kingdom of God), 5 (the boundary between the Christian and the human), and 6 (the boundary between the present and the future).

[106] Compare Hobbes' philosophy of education as necessary to curb our human inclinations, with Voltaire's *Candide,* who is naturally pure and innocent (or Daniel Defoe's character Man Friday as the naturally good indigenous person in the novel *Robinson Crusoe*—contrast William Golding's *Lord of the Flies*). The Romantic poets, such as Tennyson, have provided a welcome reaffirmation of nature. Rousseau's philosophy of education (cf. *Emile*) was one that recognized the differences between childhood and adulthood; human nature is naturally good but education is also necessary to draw it out and to enable us to develop to maturity ("Make the citizen good by training and everything else will follow"). This has also led to a revision of Darwin's theory of evolution in the realization that it was influenced by a philosophical idea of competition. More recently ecotheologians have emphasized compassion and cooperation as an equally valid understanding of evolution. See Celia Deane-Drummond, *A Primer in Ecotheology: Theology for a Fragile Earth* (Eugene, OR: Wipf and Stock, 2017).

[107] "London Taverns. The Cock" lines 71–72.

[108] *The Home We Build Together*, pp. 193ff.

[109] For a study and evaluation of theologies of work in the modern era see J. Hughes, *The End of Work: Theological Critiques of Capitalism* (Oxford: Blackwell, 2007). pp. 11ff.

[110] James Handley, "Blessed Code: How Christian ministry might be expressed through software development". *Personal Communication*, 8 October 2020, pp. 3–5.

[111] Matthew Fox, *The Reinvention of Work: A New Vision of Livelihood for Our Time* (New York: HarperCollins, 1994), p. 5. Also L. T. Johnson, *The Revelatory Body: Theology as Inductive Art*, Chapter 7 "The Body at Work", pp. 156–79 (Grand Rapids, MI: Eerdmans, 2015).

[112] H. Arendt, *The Human Condition* (Chicago: University of Chicago Press, 1998).

[113] See also the significance of the future in W. Pannenberg's programme of doing theology from below.

[114] Of course in human affairs punishment is another outcome, as a means of "bearing the blame" to use a phrase of George Herbert, from his poem "Love bade me Welcome", but that is to do with accountability and is not an alternative to forgiveness.

[115] "The life span of man running towards death would inevitably carry everything human to ruin and destruction if it were not for the faculty of interrupting it and beginning something new, a faculty which is inherent in action like an ever-present reminder that men, though they must die, are not born in order to die but to begin." (p. 246). See also Grace Jantzen, *Foundations of Violence* (Abingdon: Routledge, 2004): "Natality, creativity and beauty have been displaced, despised and ignored; at best seen as an unnecessary if pleasant extra to the real business of living." (p. 10).

[116] M. Bunting, *Willing Slaves: How the Overwork Culture is Ruling our Lives* (London: HarperCollins, 2004). See also Hurst, *Rendering Unto Caesar*, pp. 106ff.

[117] Bunting, *Willing Slaves*, p. 69.

[118] Bunting, *Willing Slaves*, p. 81.

[119] Bunting, *Willing Slaves*, pp. 71ff.

[120] Bunting, *Willing Slaves*, p. 73.

[121] Bunting, *Willing Slaves*, p. 74.

[122] Bunting, *Willing Slaves*, pp. 92–3.

[123] Bunting, *Willing Slaves*, p. 93.

[124] A. MacIntyre, *Dependent Rational Animals: Why Human Beings Need the Virtues* (London: Duckworth, 1999), p. 117. See also G. Moore, *Virtue at Work: Ethics for Individuals, Managers and Organisations* (Oxford: Oxford

University Press, 2017) for a study of A. MacIntyre's philosophy within the work setting.

[125] J. Astley, "Christian Values and the Management of Schools", in W. Kay and L. J. Francis (eds), *Religion in Education* (Leominster: Gracewing, 1998), pp. 353–86, especially p. 383. See also Bunting, *Willing Slaves*, p. 164–73: "Curiously quiet are the voices demanding to know what is the price—both to individual lives and to society—of the overwork culture. Or the voices articulating how policy and culture could encourage a broader basis for human well-being and self respect than simply a pay cheque." (p. 173); see also especially pp. 208ff.

[126] See C. Moody, *Eccentric Ministry: Pastoral Care and Leadership in the Parish* (London: Darton, Longman and Todd, 1992), pp. 83ff.

[127] So Moody, *Eccentric Ministry*, p. 83. This in turn raises a significant theme that has to do with values, especially ministry and sacrifice. These two have become almost synonymous, not least in how ministry expresses the gospel story. But it is as well to enter a caveat here in that a sacrificial value can lead to dissonance. Other values need to be weighed in the balance to ensure that self-giving is seen perspectivally and holistically.

[128] See pp. 25–26.

[129] J. Mathers, "A Healthy Society", in D. Willows and J. Swinton (eds), *Spiritual Dimensions of Pastoral Care: Practical Theology in a Multidisciplinary Context* (London: Jessica Kingsley Publishers, 2004), pp.151–7, especially p. 155. This helpfully transposes Paul's image of the Church as the body of Christ into a new register.

[130] See R. Pring, "Markets, Education and Catholic Schools", in T. H. McLaughlin, J. O'Keefe and B. O'Keeffe (eds), *The Contemporary Catholic School: Context, Identity and Diversity* (London: Falmer Press, 1996), pp. 57–9.

[131] See M. J. Whipp, *Speaking of Faith at Work: Towards a Trinitarian Hermenuetic,* PhD thesis (Glasgow University) 2008.

[132] Deirdre Palk, "God is Community", p. 4.

[133] One is reminded of a saying quoted by Martin Sawle in *Reflections on Non-Stipendiary Ministry*, ed. J. Novell, pp. 20–5, at p. 22: "The church is like a wave breaking on the beach. It only lives when it moves. As soon as it crystallizes, it begins to die."

[134] See D. E. Jenkins, "Putting Theology to Work", *Theology* 81 (1978), pp. 114–19.

135 Penny Lyon, jazz singer with "Out of the Ashes", *Church Times*, 8 March 2019, p. 56.

136 John Atherton, *Marginalization* (London: SCM Press, 2003), p. 3.

137 Sister Wendy Beckett, *The Art of Lent: A Painting a Day from Ash Wednesday to Easter* (London: SPCK, 2017), p. 12.

138 Cocksworth and Brown, *Being a Priest Today*, p. 5.

139 Ibid. p. 32.

140 Cocksworth and Brown, *Being a Priest Today*, p. 6. As Douglas Davies points out, "One challenge is to see Christian communities of faith not as places where all answers are given but where individuals commit themselves to the life of Jesus of Nazareth and to see what happens in the process, allowing working solutions to emerge from lived experience." *Private Passions: Betraying Discipleship on the Journey to Jerusalem* (Norwich: Canterbury Press, 2000), p. 46.

141 Cocksworth and Brown, *Being a Priest Today*, pp. 72ff, especially p. 73: "We always have the world with us when we worship."

142 Ibid. p. 108.

143 Ibid. pp. 173–4.

144 This is the fundamental starting point for K. Mason's study *Priesthood and Society*, and from which *mutatis mutandis* some MSEs develop a theology of priesthood within the structures of creation.

145 See Robin Bennett, "The People of God", in *Ministers of the Kingdom*, pp. 41–6. As evidence for the resilience of this particular view we may note the comments on MSE in the Report on Permanent Deacons in *For Such a Time as This: A Renewed Diaconate in the Church of England* (London: CIO, 2001), p. 60: "Looking at the matter another way, what about ordaining deacon a person who has a noted ministry, as a lay person, in their place of work? Once again, we must not appear to detract from the integrity of lay ministry and witness. We would not expect a Minister in Secular Employment to be ordained either deacon or priest unless there was a specific representative ministry of word, sacrament and pastoral care that could be discerned in that person's work situation. All Christians serve the Lord in their daily calling, whether at home, in the local community, or in another place of work. They witness to their faith in various informal ways. We would be looking for a special representative role, normally recognized in some way by the person's employer and work colleagues, before we would consider ordination

appropriate." But as we have argued, ordained ministry in the workplace enriches the ministry of the Church in the world. Moreover the evidence of MSE stories suggests that informal paths of recognition and acceptance prove effective. See note 90 and R. Williams' observation at note 186.

146 See Moody, *Eccentric Ministry*, pp. 120ff.

147 Williams, "The Christian Priest Today", p. 164.

148 "In a work environment, indeed everywhere but at the altar, every member of the worshipping community represents the Body. In a secular environment the priest has no opportunities (or at least very few) to exercise his institutional role. What he must seek to do therefore is to carry into his secular work and there express symbolically, the representative character with which he is invested in such a way that his role will be recognised by the Body as *its* role and by the world that the church comes to it as one who serves." Michael Austin in J. Fuller and P. Vaughan (eds), *Working for the Kingdom*, p. 115. See also J. Lees, *Self-Supporting Ministry*, pp. 70–1. See also R. Hacking, *On the Boundary*, pp. 83–4. See also J.M.M. Francis, "Some Reflections from the Perspective of Ministry in Secular Employment" in J. Davies (ed.) *God and the Marketplace: Essays on the Morality of Wealth Creation* (London: IEA, 1993), pp. 125–40.

149 To nurture (or grow), as compared with build (up), would draw on more organic imagery. See Francis, "A Reflection on MSE", pp. 29ff.

150 Williams et al., *Glory Descending*, p. 28.

151 Williams, *Open to Judgement*, pp. 42–4.

152 Ibid. p. 44.

153 See D. Hardy, *God's Ways With The World: Thinking and Practising Christian Faith* (Edinburgh: T. & T. Clark, 1996), pp. 195ff.

154 Williams et al., *Glory Descending*, p. 164.

155 Indeed the very act of creation itself could be conceived as hospitality i.e. God's "contraction" (note the birthing image) to give space to that which is other than God-self. See J. V. Taylor, *The Christlike God* (London: SCM Press, 1992), pp. 189–93.

156 It is also noteworthy that whilst the mention of world is frequent in the Fourth Gospel, it is mentioned ("this world") no less than forty times in the farewell discourses (predominantly under aspect (b) i.e. a qualitative distinction between the world at large and those (the disciples/the Church) chosen out of it).

[157] See C. K. Barrett, *The Gospel According to St. John* (London: SPCK, 1965), p. 135.

[158] Concerning the Johannine phrase of the Son/Jesus "being sent into the world", according to the *Theological Dictionary of the NT* Vol. III (Grand Rapids, MI: Eerdmans, 1965), p. 894, this is not just to the world of people but creation as a whole.

[159] John's Gospel speaks of the world's predicament as "not receiving" (John 1:11–12). Receiving is the counterpart of hospitality. This suggests that truth is actually something profoundly related to the establishment of community in so far as selfishness, or however the human predicament is modelled, brings with it an inability to perceive and receive truth.

[160] Corresponding metaphors in relation to God as Worker may also reflect a certain Trinitarian structure: "creating/making" as (up)building/establishing (Father); "growing/sowing" as the Word in the world (Son); "begetting, birthing" as bringing new life into being (Spirit). J. M. M. Francis, "God as Worker: A Metaphor from Daily Life in Biblical Perspective", in R. Bisschops and J. M. M. Francis (eds), *Metaphor, Canon and Community: Jewish, Christian and Islamic Approaches* (Bern: Peter Lang 1999), pp. 13–28.

[161] The feature article by Margaret Holness on the Revd William Faull (at the time vet and vicar in the Wirral) in the *Church Times*, 28 October 1994, p. 7 is remarkable and salutary in the outlining of a ministry marked by integrity in the relationship between ordination and work. (He is compared and contrasted with the fictional NSM vicar of Ambridge in *The Archers*, the Revd Robin Stokes.)

[162] J. A. T. Robinson, *On Being the Church in the World* (London: SCM Press, 1964), p. 79.

[163] We may note the language here of purity (and so of holiness) in its dedicatory significance.

[164] Robinson, *On Being the Church in the World*, p. 38.

[165] See Robinson, *On Being the Church in the World*, pp. 76–7: "The use of the word *leitourgia* (liturgy), which, like *diakonia* (deaconing), is applied also to such an economic project as the collection for the Jerusalem churches (2 Corinthians 9:12), shows how completely in early Christianity liturgy was integrated with life."

166 See Hardy, "The Future of the Church: An Exploration", in *God's Ways with the World*, p. 218. Also in the same volume, "God and the Form of Society", pp. 173ff.

167 This was advocated by John Tiller in his Report, *A Strategy for the Church's Ministry* (London: CIO, 1983), p. 103. But the Tiller Report tended, regrettably, to be seen as more about reshaping the Church managerially.

168 See Jenkins, *An Experiment in Providence*, "Community and Vocation", especially pp. 17ff.

169 Jenkins, "Community and Vocation", p. 19.

170 See especially Gage, *Priests in Secular Work: Participating in the "Missio Dei"*. Also Hurst, *Rendering unto Caesar*, pp. 111–13.

171 See E. Forshaw, "Industrial Chaplaincy and Ministry in Secular Employment" in Fuller and Vaughan *Working for the Kingdom*, pp. 67–74, especially pp. 69–70. Also P. Vaughan, *Non-Stipendiary Ministry in the Church of England: The History of the Development of an Idea* (San Francisco: Edwin Mellen, Press 1990), pp. 254ff.

172 J. Reindorp, *Equipping Christians at Work* (London: Industrial Christian Fellowship, 2000), p. 11 notes that the development of MSE in the Church "may encourage lay education in parishes, but as yet this seems more a hope than a reality". He also concludes (p. 63), "It is all too easy to allow maintenance to take over from any concept of mission."

173 See note 41.

174 Cf. Robert Langley, "Non-Stipendiary Ministry in Context", *Ministers of the Kingdom*, pp. 4–15. In this book, there seems to be an unresolved tension. Some contributors begin precisely from definitions of priesthood, e.g. p. 61 (and cf. generally pp. 52ff.): "In the ARCIC documents and the Lima text there is a recognition that 'priesthood' is a term used in a threefold way in Christian discourse." Contrast p. 11: "It will be clear, I hope, from what I have said, that I do not believe that it is possible to define ordination or priesthood and proceed from there. These concepts, I suggest, have become so bound by the particular circumstances which gave birth to them that, if we are to free what they contain, we need to start with the situation which already exists and ask in what way they resonate with it."

175 See M. Hodge, *Non-Stipendiary Ministry in the Church of England* (London: CIO, 1983), p. 60. M. Ranken, "Style and Community", in Fuller and Vaughan, *Working for the Kingdom* pp. 60ff., reflects on styles of MSE as

parish-focused (after the manner of Paul, who supported himself and built up a congregation), work-focused with an emphasis on pastoral care in the workplace, and work-focused with an awareness of prophetic engagement in the workplace. Of course such a tripartite division as this may be rather too firmly drawn.

[176]   Hardy, *God's Ways with the World*. See also Jenkins, "Putting Theology to Work", pp. 114–19.

[177]   Hardy, *God's Ways with the World*, p. 198.

[178]   Hardy, *God's Ways with the World*, pp. 200–1.

[179]   Donovan, *Christianity Rediscovered*, pp. 97, 104.

[180]   D. Hardy, *Finding the Church* (London: SCM Press, 2001), p. 39. For an exploration of how lay people articulate faith in working life see Whipp, *Speaking of Faith at Work*. See also J. A. T. Robinson, "The Christian Society and the World", in *On Being the Church in the World*, pp. 9–30.

[181]   D. Duke, "Standing on Behalf of Others", in J. M. M. Francis (ed.) *An Ordinary Way of Life: Portraits of Self-Supporting Ministry in the Diocese of Durham* (1999), pp. 29–30, especially p. 30.

[182]   See Mantle, *Britain's First Worker-Priests*, pp. 87ff.

[183]   Which remains a valid aim. See Mantle, *Britain's First Worker-Priests*, pp. 258–60.

[184]   Audenshaw Paper (See Mantle, *Britain's First Worker-Priests*, p. 258).

[185]   See D. Johnson, *A Ministers-At-Work Theology Resource Book* (1999). Jenny Gage says, "It would be good to see SSMs recognised as a fresh expression of ministry, as valid a way of being a priest as the full-time stipendiaries, in the mixed economy of the 21st century Church." "God's gift, not priest-lite cherry-pickers", *Church Times*, 2 March 2018, p. 14. See also J. Pritchard, "Ministry in Secular Employment: The Original Fresh Expression", *Ministers-at-Work: The Journal for Christians in Secular Ministry* 108 (2009), pp. 16–19. Also Betty Saunders, "Scrutiny of non-stipendiaries put in hand", *Church Times*, 26 January 1990, p. 4.

[186]   R. Gill, "Theology of the Non-Stipendiary Ministry", *Theology* 80 (1977), pp. 410–13. Johnson, "Ordained Ministers in Secular Employment", p. 24. See also R. Williams, "Ordained Ministry in the Church", *Ministers-at-Work: The Journal for Christians in Secular Ministry* 42 (1992), pp. 10–11: "Sometimes MSE is defended, or discussed, in terms of 'bringing the church into the world of work'. There are difficulties with that position. It suggests ministering

somewhere else on behalf of the church, rather than ministry to the church."
Williams' point is that MSEs should not be seen as doing something that lulls
parochial clergy into a view that this is something "heroic but quite marginal
to the church".

[187] M. Ranken, "A Theology for the Priest at Work", *Theology* 85 (1982), pp.
108–13. Michael Ranken was a priest licensed to St. Martin of Tours, Epsom;
he used his scientific work as a food technologist to explore on its own terms
the understanding of God "outside the Church", though he presented his
thinking "back to the parish".

[188] See J. Rodwell, "Blessings in Disguise". See also J. Rodwell, "Well, bless me".
The faith approach of such scientists as these responds sensitively to the
creative mystery of God in the vast majesty of the cosmos poetically expressed
e.g. in the Book of Job (Chapters 38–41).

[189] See generally M. Barker, *The Hidden Tradition of the Kingdom of God*
(London: SPCK, 2007). Mantle, *Britain's First Worker-Priests* records (p. 264)
a longing for signs of the Kingdom to emerge, and P. Baelz, in "Taking Stock",
in *Ministers of the Kingdom* (p. 88), speaks of an "incarnational" theology of
the Kingdom of God.

[190] Mantle, *Britain's First Worker-Priests*, p. 74, 94.

[191] R. Barron, *The Strangest Way: Walking the Christian Path* (Maryknoll: Orbis,
2015), p. 34.

[192] John Rodwell, "Well, bless me", *Reflections on NSM*, p. 18.

[193] Accountability, understood within mission, suggests that the Church's
understanding of new forms of ministry is best approached not from an
organizational point of view but as a theological search, in addressing change,
for how God and the world are connected. See Lees, *Self-Supporting Ministry*,
pp. 118ff.

[194] This particular value might be difficult to sustain in a world in which success
and achievement are everything. But vulnerability in ministry is a value,
success is not. On the other hand, it is not possible to be human without in
some sense acknowledging vulnerability. So this value has a place in the world
at large, however it is to be expressed. See A. Hurst, "Towards a Theology of
Paid Employment", *Expository Times* 98 (1987), pp. 260–3 for an eloquent
study of the conditions, experience and values of paid employment. It also
provides some hints relating to aspects of voluntary (i.e. unpaid) work.
He notes the significance of the values of "generosity, compassion and a

willingness to be vulnerable" (p. 262) as central to faith and the struggle to express these in the contractual obligations of work that operate with a different value set. Similarly A. Hurst, "Bridging Two Worlds", Second National Conference of Ministers in Secular Employment, Manchester, April 1986 published as a *Supplement to the Newsletter among Ministers at Work*.

[195] This involves the capacity for critical thinking. See Rodwell, "Blessings in Disguise", p. 12: "In fact it (*sc.* the church) cannot tell the world anything unless it learns intimately how to ask, how to ask the questions the world asks of itself, and how to weigh the answers which the world gives and gets Truth will, accordingly, address both veracity: what I am saying is true (as a truth claim), and sincerity: it comes from the heart." (See M. Bunting, *Willing Slaves*, p. 116).

[196] For an exercise in value discernment based upon the acronym for "Community" see M. Ranken, "Mile in My Moccasins", *Guildford Cathedral Papers*, Autumn 1990.

[197] Robert Fox, "Being MSE in Lockdown", *Ministers-at-Work: The Journal for Christians in Secular Ministry* 153 (April 2020), pp. 9–11, especially p. 11.

[198] James Sweeney, *From Story to Policy: Social Inclusion, Empowerment and the Churches* (Cambridge: Von Hügel Institute, 2001).

[199] Cited in a talk given by the Revd Canon Rosalind Brown to the Durham Diocese Ordained Local Ministers group on 4 October 2007 in which she said, "My working definition of spirituality is 'how we live our theology', but I've discovered that Joan Chittister puts it even more bluntly, 'Spirituality is theology walking.'" Henry Nouwen, *The Wounded Healer* (London: Darton, Longman and Todd, 1979), p. 89. See also Dorrie Johnson, "Spirituality for Work", *Ministers-at-Work Occasional Paper* 3 (1997). Also Peter Johnson "Making a Difference: An MSE Journey of Reflection", *Ministers-at-Work Occasional Paper* 8 (2004).

[200] J. M. Hull, "Spiritual Development: Interpretations and Applications", *British Journal of Religious Education* 24:3 (2002), p. 176.

[201] Ibid., p. 173.

[202] Grace Jantzen calls salvation flourishing. Importantly this unites inner and outer, and rescues salvation from a purely inward concern for a personal destiny. "A theology built on the model of flourishing is one whose spirituality is holistic, rather than the privatised, subjectivised spirituality so characteristic

of contemporary Christianity." "Feminism and Flourishing: Gender and Metaphor", *Feminist Theology* 18 (1995), pp. 81–101, especially p. 91.

[203] See G. S. Wakefield, *A Dictionary of Christian Spirituality* (London: SCM Press, 1983), pp. 361ff. D. Sölle, *The Silent Cry: Mysticism and Resistance* (Minneapolis: Fortress Press, 2001) affirms mysticism as bound up with the everyday, the sacred as part of the ordinariness of the world (pp. 9–22).

[204] So G. Wakefield, ibid., p. 363.

[205] For a thoughtful examination of this whole subject see G. Moore, *Virtue at Work: Ethics for Individuals, Managers and Organisations.* Also T. Keighley, *Ministry in Secular Employment (MSE) in the Church of England, 1960–2000.*

[206] M. Wedgeworth, "Priesthood and Management: A Contradiction in Terms?", in *Reflections on Non-Stipendiary Ministry*, ed. J. Novell, Diocese of Blackburn 2003, pp. 37–40, especially p. 38.

[207] See N. Vest, *Friend of the Soul: A Benedictine Spirituality of Work* (Cambridge, MA: Cowley Publications, 1997). See also Hattie Williams, "Programmers are urged to adopt good habits: Software firm pastes the Rule of St. Benedict into its Code of Conduct", *Church Times*, 26 October 2018, p. 2.

[208] See Johnson, *Spirituality for Work.* The booklet includes helpful quotations, a reading list, and a series of language parallels between the discourse of faith and work. See also D. Johnson, *A Ministers-At-Work Theology Resource Book*, which structures theological and spiritual reflection as a series of questions in a jigsaw framework. See also K. Holt, "Towards a Framework for Spirituality", *Ministers-at-Work: The Journal for Christians in Secular Ministry* 44 (December 1992), pp. 8–10. See also Thornton, "The Ministry of Prayer", in Baelz and Jacob (eds), *Ministers of the Kingdom*, pp. 66–74 (particularly for a Benedictine understanding), and also T. Pitt, "Spirituality and the MSE", *Ministers-at-Work: The Journal for Christians in Secular Ministry* 33 (1990), pp. 9–11.

[209] Archbishop K. Rayner, *Ordained Ministry in Secular Employment: Reflections on the History and Theology*, ACCM Occasional Paper 31 (1989), pp. 25–43 especially p. 42.

[210] S. Yore, *The Mystic Way in Postmodernity: Transcending Theological Boundaries in the Writings of Iris Murdoch, Denise Levertov and Annie Dillard* (Bern: Peter Lang, 2009), p. 122. This would be the underlying perspective of the claim: "God has no hands but our hands . . . etc." See also bShabbat 10a, 119b God invites his people at Sinai to be his "partners in the work of creation". See

Sacks, *The Home We Build Together*, p. 109, " ... there is one thing God cannot do alone, namely live within the human heart: for that he depends on the willingness of humans." This perhaps explains why, if Christianity values God's presence towards the world as grace, Judaism values freedom as the core of the relationship between God and humanity (ibid. p. 105).

211   *The Christian Universe* (London: Darton, Longman and Todd, 1996), p. 91, and quoted in Thornton, "The Ministry of Prayer", in Baelz & Jacob (eds), *Ministers of the Kingdom*, pp. 67-8. See also R. S. Thomas, "Suddenly (after long silence)", *Collected Poems 1945-1990* (London: Phoenix 1993) p. 426. Also J. Philip Newell, *The Book of Creation: The Practice of Celtic Spirituality* (Norwich: Canterbury Press, 1999), Introduction, pp. xv-xxv.

212   *Best of Blue*, p. 135. As Hugh Valentine puts it: "I have always had an interest in how the gospel relates to lived human experience—the vast majority of which occurs beyond the church-as-building." "How and why I became an SSM", in Lees, *Self-Supporting Ministry*, "Called to the Margins", p. 51.

213   "Work that Enfaiths", in *New and Selected Essays* (New York: New Directions, 1992), p. 251.

214   Keith Rayner, *Ordained Ministry in Secular Employment: Reflections on the History and Theology*, ACCM Occasional Paper no. 31 (1989), p. 38.

215   See A. Larive, *After Sunday: A Theology of Work* (London: Continuum, 2004), p. 38.

216   P. Evdokimov, "La sacerdoce universel des laics dans la tradition orientale", in Elchinger, L. A. (ed.), *L'Eglise en Dialogue* (Paris, 1962), pp. 39-40, and cited in Cocksworth and Brown, *Being a Priest Today*, pp. 191, 235.

217   *Centuries of Meditations* (The Second Century, 97.1-3). It is also worth noting a comment by Rabbi Lionel Blue that "the secular world is more spiritual than it thinks, just as the ecclesiastical world is more materialist than it cares to acknowledge".

218   Modern business has picked up on the place of imagination in the workplace, even if it is also true that many work contexts lack opportunity to value imagination. This could be seen as essentially a wish to improve the profitability of work, but deep down it is probably better to accept that this is in fact an acceptance in a genuine sense of the need for imagination in human flourishing. There is scope aplenty here for an holistic understanding of work for an MSE's presence within the workplace. Part of this will be to help to discern what might be simply aspirational and what is realistic in good

3:4

working practices. See J. O'Donohue, *Anam Cara: Spiritual Wisdom from the Celtic World* (London: Bantam Books, 1999), pp. 162ff.

[219] See also the earlier reflection on the dimensions of breadth, length, height and depth in Chapter 3.

[220] J. Fraser, "MSE—A Ministry in Sex Employment?", in *You Do What? Stories of Non-Stipendiary Ministers in the Diocese of Worcester* (2012), pp. 19–22, especially p. 22.

[221] K. Rahner, *Faith in a Wintry Season* (New York: Crossroad, 1990), p. 115.

[222] J. Inge, *A Christian Theology of Place* (Abingdon: Routledge, 2016), p. 2.

[223] So Ted Wragg on cutting back on bureaucracy: "Bureaucracy is a symptom, not a cause. Trying to prune it is like giving earplugs to the driver of a noisy car, instead of replacing the clapped-out engine. The endemic disease in education is lack of trust . . . Unless real trust were fully restored, such cosmetics (*sc.* cutting the mountain of forms) would not affect one jot the climate of suspicion that has bedevilled relationships between governments and schools for two decades" (4 June 2002, cited in *The Guardian* (E Supplement) 15 November, 2005, pp. 1–2).

[224] Margaret Trivasse, "Where is 'the Touching Place' now?", *Ministers-at-Work: The Journal for Christians in Secular Ministry* 154 (July 2020), pp. 16–18, especially pp. 17–18.

[225] T. S. Eliot, "Burnt Norton" (ii), *Four Quartets* (London: Faber, 1959).

[226] See the Japanese art of *kintsugi* as a method of repairing in gold, and thereby honouring the history of broken pottery.

[227] See R. S. Thomas' poem "The Bright Field", *Collected Poems 1945–1990* (London: Phoenix, 1993), p. 302 and the insistence in "must" (as also in the conclusion of George Herbert's poem "Love bade me welcome").

[228] Jean Skinner, "Not Quite Kosher", *Personal Communication*, 1 October 1999, pp. 6, 8.

[229] T. Merton, *Contemplative Prayer* (Garden City, NY: Doubleday Image, 1971), p. 39.

[230] See René Voillaume, *Brothers of Men: Letters to the Petits Frères* (London: Darton, Longman and Todd, 1966).

[231] See D. Levertov, *The Poet in the World* (New York: New Directions, 1973) p. 8.

[232] See Sallie McFague, *Super, Natural Christians* (Minneapolis: Fortress Press, 1997), pp. 28, 149; also her *Life Abundant* (Minneapolis: Fortress Press, 2001) for the challenges to the world faced in post-modernity.

233   Barbara Brown Taylor, *An Altar in the World* (Norwich: Canterbury Press, 2009), p. 115.

234   Sallie McFague, *Speaking in Parables: A Study in Metaphor and Theology* (Philadelphia: Fortress Press, 1975), p. 66.

235   A-J. Levine and M. Z. Brettler, *The Jewish Annotated New Testament (NRSV)* (Oxford: Oxford University Press, 2011), p. 381.

236   See the overarching narrative of Peter Johnson in *Priest of the Profane*.

237   See R. Williams, *Anglican Identities*, pp. 4, 7.

238   Michael Powell, "Playing Cards: Making Connections", *Personal Communication*, 24 October 1999, pp. 7–8.

239   In the Greek of John 1.14 the word for "dwelt" is "*eskénōsen*" (from the word "skéné" = tent), and which in turn in its consonants echoes the Hebrew word "sheckinah" (the dwelling of the divine Presence of God).

240   Jim Cummins, "The Holiness of the Mundane", *Personal Communication*, 8 August 1999, pp. 1–14, especially p. 1.

241   David E. Jenkins, "Christian Faith in God", in *Still Living with Questions* (London: SCM Press, 1990), p. 34.

242   Rowan Williams, *Being Human: Bodies, Minds, Persons* (London: SPCK, 2018), pp. 110–11.

243   See C. E. Raven, *Science, Religion and the Future* (Cambridge: Cambridge University Press, 2008), pp. 30, 41–2. Sallie McFague points out that the parables of Jesus bring together the mundane and the sacred. See her *Metaphorical Theology: Models of God in Religious Language* (Philadelphia: Fortress Press, 1982), pp. 46–7. Also Sallie McFague *Speaking in Parables*, p. xvii.

244   Psalm 104 and Job 38–41 reflect different, though not unrelated views of nature.

245   See Francis, "Nature Untamed: Reflections from Scripture".

246   Toil and labour in the Graeco-Roman world were not despised because that was the work of slaves but because that work signalled a life constrained by necessity, and thus required slaves to do it. Consequently, for Plato, "a poor man is not master of himself" (Seventh Letter 351A). At Luke 16:3 the unjust steward eschews working not because it is beneath him (that he reserves for begging) but because of his age and lack of physical strength. See Johnson *The Revelatory Body* pp.158–164.

[247] Cf. Proverbs 8:30, although the variant reading of heavenly Wisdom as "a little child" (RSV footnote) rather than a master craftsman would give a different vision of the divine creativity. See Francis, "God as Worker: A Metaphor in Biblical Perspective", pp. 13–28.

[248] This passage draws on an Egyptian writing called "The Satire of the Trades". This work satirizes daily work in comparison with the scribe. The Book of Wisdom is more nuanced, describing trades as important in society, albeit that this limits the time given to the study of the Law. Thus the vocation of the scribe is the best work of all.

[249] See J. Eaton, *The Contemplative Face of Old Testament Wisdom (in the Context of World Religions)* (London: SCM Press, 1989), pp. 70–6.

[250] See A. E. Harvey, "The workman is worthy of his hire: fortunes of a proverb in the early church", *Novum Testamentum* 24 (1982), pp. 209–21.

[251] The story of John 21 in its parallel with Luke 5 suggests that Peter had gone back to his occupation as a fisherman, portraying him as someone who had once been an apostle and had become a fisherman, as distinct from someone who had been a fisherman and had become an apostle. Thus the story in John is of the reawakening of Peter's vocation. See Eamon Duffy, "The Fish Breakfast", in *Walking to Emmaus* (London: Burns & Oates, 2006), pp. 41–9. See also K. C. Hanson, "The Galilean Fishing Economy and the Jesus Tradition", *Biblical Theology Bulletin* 27 (1997), pp. 99–111.

[252] R. Hock now favours the necessity of embarking on the Gentile mission as the fundamental reason for Paul's taking up a tentmaking trade. R. Hock, "The Problem of Paul's Social Class: Further Reflections", in *Paul's World*, ed. S. Porter (Leiden: E. J. Brill, 2008), pp. 7–18. See also G. Theissen, "Legitimation and subsistence: an essay on the sociology of early Christian missionaries", in *The Social Setting of Pauline Christianity* (Edinburgh: T. &. T. Clark, 1982), pp. 35ff. For a detailed contextual study see H-A. M. Hartley, *We worked night and day that we might not burden any of you (1 Thessalonians 2.9): Aspects of the Portrayal of Work in the Letters of Paul, Late Second Temple Judaism, the Graeco-Roman World and Early Christianity*, DPhil Thesis, Oxford University, 2004.

[253] See M. Hengel, *The Pre-Christian Paul* (London: SCM Press, 1991), pp. 15ff.

[254] See R. Hock, *The Social Context of Paul's Ministry: Tentmaking and Apostleship* (Philadelphia: Fortress Press, 1980), pp. 52ff.

255 See R. Hock, "Paul's Tentmaking and the Problem of His Social Class", *Journal of Biblical Literature* 97 (1978), pp. 558–62; P. Green, *The Hellenistic Age: A Short History* (New York: The Modern Library, 2008), pp. 53–4: "All manual labour and trade was despised as 'banausic', a term originally meaning 'to do with handicrafts' but soon equated with anything lower-class, common, or in bad taste."; cf. pp. 98–9: " . . . the virulently antibanausic class-prejudice that permeated Greek society of all periods". See also Marcus Sidonius Falx with Jerry Toner, *How To Manage Your Slaves* (London: Profile Books, 2015), pp. 4, 11, 79–80. As the gap between rich and poor widened, and attitudes to have-nots hardened, including (under Roman influence) slaves, (Green, ibid. pp. 75–6), it is little wonder that Paul as an apostle encountered resistance to his self-support amongst elites. Some have found hints of this in what the prophet Amos says about his own background as a shepherd (Amos 1:1). See R. Picardo, *Ministry Makeover: Recovering a Theology for Bi-Vocational Service in the Church* (Eugene, OR: Wipf & Stock, 2015), pp. 23–7.

256 See C. Maurer, "Grund und Grenze apostolischer Freiheit: exegetisch-theologische Studie zu 1 Korinther 9", in *Antwort: Festschrift zum 70. Geburtstag von Karl Barth* (Zollikon-Zurich: Evangelischer Verlag AG, 1956), pp. 630–64. See also generally J. Murphy-O'Connor, *Paul: A Critical Life* (Oxford: Oxford University Press, 1996), and *Paul: His Story* (Oxford: Oxford University Press, 2003), pp. 28ff., and N. T. Wright, *Paul: A Biography* (London: SPCK, 2018), pp. 11, 15, 68–9.

257 We may note how Prisca is mentioned first, as likely the key figure in the business. Women could hold business status in the Ancient World.

258 See J. D. G. Dunn, *The Epistle to the Galatians* (London: A. & C. Black, 1993), p. 328.

259 G. W. Lampe considers whether the emergence of a supported ministry was actually instrumental in the ministry of the Church turning aside from engagement with the world. "Secularisation in the New Testament and the Early Church", *Theology* 71 (April 1968), pp. 163–75.

260 This resonates with 1 Corinthians 9:14–15, and it contributes an insight to why Paul did not himself follow the commandment of Jesus but chose instead a self-supporting ministry. This did not mean (contrary, no doubt, to some comments at Corinth) that Paul was insufficiently committed to God (Providence) in trusting himself wholeheartedly to the support of the Church. As these verses from Philippians confirm, Paul trusted fully in God's

providential care in Christ. His following a self-supporting ministry is not about abandoning dependency on God—he is at one with Jesus in this. But it is, as a further motivating principle, about offering the Gospel "free of charge". This is consistent with Paul's pragmatism where 1 Corinthians 9:18 is not a matter of disobedience but a voluntary adjustment in terms of not accepting a full right due to him, which action is itself informed by another good principle.

261 See Vaughan, "An Historical Perspective", pp. 121–2.

262 As claimed by Vaughan, "An Historical Perspective", pp. 129–30.

263 Assuming that Pauline authorship applies to both.

264 See R. Hock, "The Workshop as a Social Setting for Paul's Missionary Preaching", *Catholic Biblical Quarterly* 41:3 (1979), pp. 438–50.

265 So rightly Hacking, *On the Boundary*, pp. 8–9.

266 The "we" that Paul uses e.g. 1 Thessalonians 2:9 would have included his companions, Timothy, Titus, Silas and Barnabas (1 Corinthians 9:6). Prisca and Aquila were likewise missionaries who shared Paul's trade.